CLIMBING THE MOUNTAIN

The Journey of Prayer

For Tom and Jo, *meum et tuum*

CLIMBING THE MOUNTAIN

The Journey of Prayer

James Tolhurst

GRACEWING

First published in 2010

Gracewing
2 Southern Avenue
Leominster
Herefordshire HR6 0QF

All rights reserved. No part of this publication may be reproduced, stored in a retrieval system, or transmitted in any form, or by any means, electronic, mechanical, photo copying, recording or otherwise, without the written permission of the publisher.

© James Tolhurst 2010

The right of James Tolhurst to be identified as the author of this work has been asserted in accordance with the Copyright, Designs and Patents Act 1988.

ISBN 978 0 85244 372 9

Typeset by Action Publishing Technology Ltd
Gloucester GL1 5SR

Contents

Preface by *Archbishop John J. Myers*   ix
Introduction   xiii

Chapter 1	Before we pray: 'Enter into your secret room'	1
	'Go to your private room'	2
	A time for prayer	3
	Even if God does not give us what we ask	4
	Prepare to pray	5
	'Make yourself aware'	6
	Praying for assistance	7
Chapter 2	Begin to pray: 'The Spiritual Combat'	9
	Repentance	10
	Detachment	11
	Distractions	13
Chapter 3	The Sources of Prayer	16
	The Word of God	16
	Praying with a book ...	20
	The Passion of Christ	21
	The lives of the saints	22
	The *Our Father*	23
	Other prayers	23

	The rosary	24
	The Eucharist	25
	Additional helps	26
Chapter 4	The Saints and Spiritual Writers – 1	28
	The apostolic age	28
	The Eastern Fathers	30
	The power of fasting	31
	Into the darkness	32
	In the image of God ...	34
	Voices from the West	35
	Augustine (354–430)	37
	The *Devotio Moderna*	39
	The Cloud of Unknowing	41
	Two saints from Spain	42
Chapter 5	The Saints and Spiritual Writers – 2	47
	St Francis de Sales	47
	St Ignatius	48
	Brother Lawrence	51
	Fr John Nicholas Grou	52
	More recent times	54
	Abbot Columba Marmion	54
	Dom Anselm Rutherford	56
	St Josemaría Escrivá de Balaguer	57
	Fr Yves Raguin	58
	The *Catechism of the Catholic Church*	59

Contents vii

Chapter 6	Pray as You Can and Not as You Can't	63
	Meditation	63
	The Jesus Prayer	67
	Unceasing prayer	69
	Prayer of the present moment	71
	Vocal prayers	72
Chapter 7	Climbing the Mountain	75
	Aridity in prayer	75
	The first 'night'	76
	Consolations	79
	Spiritual direction	81
Chapter 8	The Heights of Prayer	85
	Entering into the 'night'	85
	The dark night of the soul	86
	Desolation	88
	The fire of God's love	90
	The night of faith	90
Chapter 9	The Living Flame of Love	94
	Theosis or deification	97
	The living flame of love	99
	'He who is joined to God becomes one spirit with him'	102
Chapter 10	Certain Mystical Experiences	104
	Ecstasy	104
	Revelations and visions	107
	Intellectual revelations	110
	Other mystical phenomena	111

Chapter 11 A Wondrous Journey   115

Select Bibliography   119
Appendix 1: Meditation Methods   125
Appendix 2: Prayers   129

Note
Scripture references are taken from the RSV Bible, the North American Bible and the Jerusalem Bible.

Preface

Fr James Tolhurst continues his significant reflections on various aspects of our life in Christ. *Climbing the Mountain: The Journey of Prayer* is a very welcome addition to these. It is essential for us today to realize that life is more than the frenzied bustle of activity in which we all sometimes find ourselves. We must begin with the interior life. To lay upon oneself or others the burden of being authentic disciples of Jesus Christ without rooting that discipleship in the interior life is an impossibility. With that, Fr Tolhurst makes clear that setting aside time and space for prayer is an important beginning. He makes clear also that it is not easily done, that there are a variety of obstacles – which he helps us to identify. Since prayer is a gift of the Holy Spirit and given within the context of our life in the Church, which is the Body of Christ, it is important to recognize the various sources of prayer which the Holy Spirit makes available to us.

Fr Tolhurst makes us aware that the journey to a rich prayer life will involve such things as aridity or dryness. He also reminds us that part of the difficulty is our own 'darkness' which is associated with incomprehension and blindness.

The news is not all bad. There are consolations which

can be both physically and spiritually experienced and which are to be savoured when the Lord grants them. We should thank God when we have this gift but we should know that prayer is possible without such consolations. St John of the Cross reflects on the desire for quiet reflection, 'A person likes to remain alone in loving awareness of God, without particular considerations, interior peace and quiet may pose, without the acts of exercises ... of the intellect memory and will; and that the first remain only in the general, loving awareness and knowledge that we mentioned, without any particular knowledge or understanding.'

Climbing the Mountain: The Journey of Prayer is a fine book drawing from many rich sources in the life of the Church and the lives of great spiritual leaders. I commend it to those who are undertaking a serious prayer life for the first time and to those who are looking for a fresh beginning in their own lives of prayer.

+ Most Reverend John J. Myers
Archbishop of Newark

While my soul like a white palmer
Travels to the land of heaven,
Over the silver mountains.
Sir Walter Raleigh

Introduction

The psalmist begs, 'Send forth your light and your truth; let these be my guide. Let them bring me to your holy mountain, to the place where you dwell' (Ps. 42:3). We cannot pray without divine help, because in prayer we aim for nothing less than God himself.

There is always a danger in books about prayer that they are too technical. Brother Lawrence (who had been a footman, but 'a great awkward fellow who broke everything') remarks, 'Having found in many books different methods of going to God, and divers practices of the spiritual life, I thought this would serve rather to puzzle me than facilitate what I sought after, which was nothing but how to become wholly God's.'[1] Prayer cannot be seen as a spiritual workout or mind game but rather as a journey, in which we confide our mind and heart to God who leads us to his holy mountain.

St Teresa of Avila – an extraordinary woman in so many respects – talks expansively of her experiences in prayer (fortunately for us). She is an enthusiastic proponent, 'Anyone who has not begun to pray, I beg for the love of the Lord not to miss so great a blessing.'[2] In the following pages, you will find her words backed up by witnesses from Eastern and Western Christianity: from earliest times to the modern day.

Cardinal Newman says, 'Whereas the faith is everywhere one and the same ... a large liberty is accorded to private judgement and inclination as regards matters of devotion.'[3] This would apply especially to prayer. We are completely free to choose how and when we pray and we should vigorously defend our rights in this respect. As the Spanish Carmelite puts it, 'Jesus says to all, "If any man thirsts let him come to me and drink" but he gives his water *in many ways* to those who try to follow him.'[4]

This is meant not only to apply to the methods we use to help us to pray but also to let us know how liberal are the graces which God will give us when we pray. But as prayer is a journey we move into unexplored territory, and 'It is not enough to move onwards, one must also see where one is going! "Progress" does not suffice, if there are no criteria as reference points.'[5] Those who have made the journey have left us just such indications. They talk about the struggle to pray, which is so dispiriting for many, 'rejecting wounding thoughts and falling back into them'.[6] They talk about the nature of the consolations that God gives to encourage us and what our attitude should be; and that period when meditation becomes impossible and later when it seems 'darkness' descends. Above all they remind us of the value of being with God during this time, and the power of his presence, 'Believe me, count as loss each day you have not used in loving God.'[7]

God does call some to the heights of prayer and there are indications about that as well. It is not granted to all, but it is possible that the invitation is more widely offered and not being taken up. We are secretly suspicious of 'spiritual' people. Some we have met seem to combine spirituality with a rather joyless irritability. It is a case of the little girl's prayer, 'Lord, please make all bad people good, and all good people nice.' God does not call everyone to the heights but he may call you and you should be open to the possibility; says St Teresa, 'Dispose yourself for contemplation ...'[8]

But at the same time, you need to know what you are letting yourself in for. This is the living God, a mountain that might be touched, and 'a burning fire, and a whirlwind, and darkness and gloom ...' (Heb. 12:18). Moses was asked to take off his shoes when he confronted the burning bush ...

Prayer is meant to have a profound effect on our lives. Indeed the lack of prayer could be seen at the root of so much sorrow; Monica Baldwin ('I Leapt over the Wall') courageously admitted to not praying enough.[9] Jesus has left us the example of whole nights spent in prayer.

Those who talk in terms of religion being a matter of established theology or the performance of certain external acts need to understand that these are all profoundly rooted in our living and personal relationship with the God who loves us. Be convinced, as was William Law (1686–1761) when he wrote:

> Sometimes the light of God's countenance shines so brightly upon us, we see so far into the invisible world, we are so affected with the wonders of the love and goodness of God that our hearts worship and adore in a language that is higher than that of words and we feel transports of devotion which only can be imagined.[10]

There is undoubtedly a renewed interest in our spiritual side which has been aroused lately by a greater acquaintance with Oriental mysticism; unfortunately it is often a fad which people soon tire of. It is, however, an irony that in England and Wales, the idea of Christian prayer is seldom considered; yet in the Middle Ages there were 800 religious houses where it was a daily practice. Christian prayer needs to be discovered, or in many cases, rediscovered – it is that mountain waiting to be climbed.

James Tolhurst
Advent 2009

Notes
1. Brother Lawrence (1605–1691), 12th Letter, p. 56.
2. *Life*, chapter 8.
3. Newman, J. H. (1801–1890), *Difficulties of Anglicans 2* (preached when vicar of St Mary's), vol. 2, p. 30.
4. *Way of Perfection*, chapter 17.
5. Benedict XVI, Homily, 22 May 2008.
6. Brother Lawrence, 2nd Conversation, p. 24.
7. *Way of Perfection*, chapter 40.
8. Ibid., chapter 19.
9. *The Times*, 5 January 1968.
10. William Law (1686–1761): Nonjuror and spiritual writer. Quoted in Fanning, p. 183.

Chapter 1

Before we pray: 'Enter into your secret room'

Much to the disgust of Horatio, Hamlet is unrepentant, 'For every man hath business and desire. Such as it is, - and for my own poor part, look you, I'll go pray.'[1] Prayer for most of human history has been a part of everyday existence. Only recently has it become an option like aerobics or jogging.

Prayer has been defined 'as the raising up of the mind and heart to God'.[2] But this almost implies some special technique. When St John Vianney found one of the farmers of his village in church absorbed in prayer, he asked him, 'What are you doing here all this time?' The farmer replied, 'I look at the good God and he looks at me.' He was subsequently to tell his congregation, 'Everything is in that, my children.'[3] Prayer is that communion with God, of mind and heart. It is a conversation that does not need words in which we turn to God, the author of all that is, the wellspring of our very being. The psalmist is talking of prayer when he says, 'As the deer that yearns for running streams, so my soul is yearning for you, my God. My soul is thirsting for God, the God of my life' (Ps. 42:2-3). Prayer is part of that thirst which we should all feel. St John Chrysostom says, 'I speak of prayer, not words. It is the longing for God, love too deep for words, a gift not given to humanity but by God's grace ...'[4] If there is not the habit of prayer, it is because the idea of God as a living reality has grown dim in many hearts. Without at least a desire for God, the concept of prayer becomes meaningless. But with only the smallest spark of desire, there is that awareness of the need to respond as the weather vane can turn with the slightest wind.

'Go to your private room'

In the long passage which Matthew relates under the title 'The Sermon on the Mount', Jesus talks about the practice of prayer, 'When you pray, enter into your inner chamber, and, when you have shut your door, pray to your Father who is in that secret place ...' (Matthew 6:6).

We notice that during his life on earth, Jesus drew aside to pray. We are told 'he prayed alone' (Luke 9:18), 'he withdrew to the wilderness and prayed' (Luke 5:16), 'he went into the hills by himself to pray' (Matthew 14:2:3) and he 'withdrew to a lonely place' (Mark 1:35). This, in spite of the fact that he was always in the presence of his Father, 'He who sent me is always with me; he has not left me alone' (John 8:29).

There is a need to withdraw to some secret place (ταμεῖον is called a hiding place in Matthew 24:26) where we can be alone with God. In his humanity Jesus, despite being one with the Father, experienced that need to distance himself from the turmoil of daily life so that he could pray. Prayer cannot simply be turned on like a tap because we fancy a bit of spirituality. It requires preparation – we must go into our private room. There must be some physical detachment. Origen says, 'In order that each person may say his prayers in peace and without distraction, there is also a command to select in one's house if possible the so-called holiest place and ... to pray there.'[5] In his *Rule* St Benedict recommends the Oratory of the monastery, 'If anyone should wish to pray secretly, let him just go in and pray, not in a loud voice but with tears and fervour of heart.'[6]

The Acts of the Apostles tells us that Peter, following the practice of pious Jews who prayed three times a day (cf. Dan 6:10), 'went up to the housetop at about the sixth hour to pray' (Acts 10:9). Cardinal Lercaro, weighing up the merits of church or inner room for prayer, opts for the latter because he says that 'The place to be chosen is that where there is least likelihood of meeting with distractions or interruptions.'[7] There is a peculiar guilt about wanting to be alone which could almost be called the Garbo syndrome. In fact we need to be alone if we are to pray. We cannot be alone if our mind is elsewhere. We need to be with God.

A time for prayer

It seems almost against the spirit of prayer to insist on a particular time – as if we are pressuring the Holy Spirit and confining the grace of God to a timetable. Nevertheless, for our own sake, we need to budget a time for prayer each day or we will neglect it. We ought to reflect that we are created by a loving God and prayer is that constant, daily reminder, 'Stated times of prayer put us in that posture (as I may call it) in which we ought ever to be.'[8]

There is no hard and fast rule about the exact time we should choose. Some authors recommend the morning. St

Francis de Sales was in favour of 'some time or other before the midday meal, because your mind will be less distracted and more refreshed after the repose of the night'.[9] Others say that the evening has decided advantages. Whatever we decide, we should stick to it. St Vincent de Paul says it is 'a daily bread, a manna which must be gathered every day'.[10] This also applies to the time we give to prayer. On the one hand Padre Pio says that we should be faithful to our resolution to the time we allocate, 'Make a meditation of patience; you will profit all the same. Fix the time, the length of your meditation, and do not rise from your place until you have finished it.'[11] On the other hand St Teresa of Avila insists, 'We must shorten our time of prayer, however much joy it gives us, if we see our bodily strength waning or find our head aches: discretion is most necessary in everything.'[12] St Teresa was thinking of her Sisters with their frequent psychosomatic illnesses, which she allowed for. St John Chrysostom, in the midst of pastoral struggles, makes the point about *perseverance* in prayer, 'Even if God does not immediately give us what we ask, even if lots of people try to put us off our prayers, still let us go on praying.'[13]

Even if God does not give us what we ask ...

It is no good thinking that like exercises in the gym, we will get something out of prayer. Prayer cannot really be measured on any human scale. We should not pray because of the satisfaction we hope to obtain. Prayer should be a surrender of ourselves to God. Cassian insists, 'Perfect prayer is that wherein he who prays is not conscious that he is praying.'[14] Julian of Norwich goes further, 'Pray wholeheartedly, though you may feel nothing, though you think that you could not, for in dryness and in barrenness; in sickness and in weakness, then is your prayer most pleasing.'[15]

We should not be put off by a feeling of reluctance – prayer has to *become* part of our daily routine; and the 'learning process' will take time. You have to *want* to pray – even if there are conflicting emotions – and to be willing to make the effort.

Prepare to pray

But before engaging in prayer you need to *prepare*. Cassian says,

> We must put ourselves in the state of mind we would wish to have in us when we actually pray ... The soul will rise to the heights of heaven or plunge into the things of earth, depending upon where it lingered before the time of prayer.[16]

The early Christian writers were strongly of the opinion that 'prayer has the labour of a mighty conflict to one's last breath'.[17] The conflict is above all with our own nature, although the Desert Fathers spoke of a warfare masterminded by the evil spirits, 'those who are entrusted with the appetites of gluttony, those who suggest avaricious thoughts, and those who incite us to seek the esteem of men'.[18] When we pray we lay ourselves open and reveal our hidden weaknesses. If we are conscious of any evil inclinations or sins which remain unrepented, our conscience will remind us of their presence. Cassian says,

> First of all suppress any kind of desire for the things of the flesh ... Next, renounce evil speaking, vain words, long high-sounding discourses, scurrilous witticisms, conquer the

agitation that comes from anger or melancholy. Cut off greed and attachment to money at the roots.[19]

Prayer cannot be undertaken lightly as a veneer to a life which is displeasing to God. The author of *The Cloud of Unknowing* says,

> You must constantly revert to these two words in turn, 'Sin' and 'God'. With the knowledge that if you had God you would not have sin, and if you had not sin, then you would have God ... If you were to ask me when [to engage in contemplation], I would answer, 'not before they have cleansed their conscience of all their past sins'.[20]

St Alphonsus who had considerable experience in directing the spiritual life maintained, 'Sin may coexist with all other exercises of piety; but prayer and sin cannot possibly dwell together, the soul will abandon prayer or sin.'[21]

There is a somewhat brutal fact which we need to face in our lives: if we wish to be committed to God and to a life of prayer we cannot try to serve two masters (Matthew 6:24). But, once having renounced sin, 'One has only to stretch out one's hands and say, "Lord, as you will" and "have mercy on me".'[22]

'Make yourself aware'

When Moses turned aside to see the burning bush, God said to him, 'Do not come near; put off your shoes from your feet, for the place on which you are standing is holy ground ... And Moses hid his face, for he was afraid to look at God' (Exo 3:4.6). Prayer involves us in this encounter with the living God, and with us our consciousness of our dependence on him. Brother Lawrence says, 'His prayer was simply the presence of God, his soul unconscious of all else but love.'[23] We have to face up to fact that God is always near to us, 'but we are far from him. God is within; we are without. God is at home; we are abroad'[24] or as Augustine put it, 'You were with me but I was not with you.'[25] This by no means excludes a true and living conversation, as took place between God and Moses for instance, 'as a man talks with his friend' (Exo 33:11). St Teresa remarks, 'Who is there to prevent you from turning the eyes of your soul, though it be but for a moment, if you can do no more, upon the Lord?'[26] This practice of the presence of God is an indispensable introduction to true prayer because it makes us vividly aware of the one to whom we pray and arouses in us that feeling, 'Lord, it is good for us to be here with you' (cf. Luke 9:33).

Praying for assistance

We should not neglect to pray for assistance (a list of prayers is given in Appendix 2) from the Holy Spirit, together with Our Lady and the saints that our time will not be wasted. It is as well to remind ourselves that we will always be sinners in need of the mercy of God and we come into his presence with humility, knowing that he loves us and has called us to be with him in this special time. St Theodorus tells us,

> It is clear therefore that he who loves God desires always to be with him and to converse with him. This comes to pass in us through pure prayer. Accordingly, let us apply ourselves to pray with all our power, for it enables us to become akin to God. Such a man was he who said, 'O God, my God, I cry to you at dawn, my soul thirsts for you.'(Ps. 63:1)[27]

And, what if there is still that reluctance to pray? Evagrius remarks, 'If you have not yet received the charism of prayer ... then ask perseveringly, and you will receive.'[28]

Notes

1. *Hamlet*, Act 1, Scene 4.
2. John Damascene (675–749), *De Fide Orthodoxa*, 3, 24, PG 94.1089.
3. Trochu, *Curé of Ars*, p. 184.
4. Homily 6, *De Predicatione*, PG 64.465.
5. Origen, *de Oratione*, 31.4; St Bernard comments, 'The bridegroom, the Lord of the universe, makes plans and works from a distant, secret place' (*On the Song of Songs* n. 3).
6. *Rule*, chapter 52.
7. Lercaro, p. 207.
8. Newman, *Parochial & Plain Sermons*, vol. 1, p. 249.
9. *Introduction to the Devout Life*, Book 2, chapter 1.
10. D'Agnel, pp. 72–7.
11. *Counsels*.
12. *Way of Perfection*, chapter 26.
13. *Homily on Matthew*, 66, 1.
14. *Conference 9*
15. Julian of Norwich (1342–1413) *14th Revelation* p. 41.
16. *Conference 9*.
17. Abba Agatho, *Sayings*.
18. Evagrius, *Texts on Discrimination in respect of Passions & Thoughts*, 1.
19. *Conference 9*.
20. Chapter 40.
21. Alphonsus Liguori (1696–1787), vol. 9, n. 3, p. 217.
22. Abba Makarios, *The Raising of the Intellect*, n. 19.
23. *Practice of the Presence of God*, *4th Conversation*, p. 29.
24. Meister Eckhart, *Sermon 6*, p. 132.
25. *Conferences*, 10.
26. *Way of Perfection*, chapter 28.
27. Theodorus the Great Ascetic, *A Century of Spiritual Texts*, n. 94.
28. *De Oratione*, n. 87.

Chapter 2

Begin to pray: 'The Spiritual Combat'

> The battle you are to fight is within you ...Your enemy comes out of your own heart.
>
> Origen, *Moralia in Job*

Cardinal Newman was no stranger to the difficulties of prayer. He wrote in a meditation,

> I love anything better than communion with [God]. Often I find it difficult even to say my prayers. There is hardly any amusement I would not rather take up than set myself to think of you. Give me grace, my Father to be utterly ashamed of my own reluctance.[1]

We have already touched on the 'labour' involved in praying. The early Fathers of the Church talk in terms of a spiritual combat and prayer as the weapon in the fight, 'Unless we are armed with it, we cannot be engaged in warfare, but are carried off as prisoners to the enemy's country.'[2] Prayer involves us in serious work and lays bare our deepest motivations and desires. Sirach says bluntly, 'If you come forward to serve the Lord, prepare yourself for temptation' (Sir 2:1). Early practitioners carried out this 'service' by going into the desert of Egypt to do battle with their passions and temptations and to be alone with God. St Anthony the Abbot (251–356) whose life was written by St Athanasius, is the most famous. His years of asceticism did not shorten his life . . .

The Desert Fathers have left us a great assortment of aphorisms based on their experiences. If we wish to enter into that 'combat' we need to call upon God's help and mean what we pray: 'Hear my words, O Lord; listen to my sighing' (Ps. 5:2); 'Lord, show me the way of salvation'; 'Lord, have mercy on me, as you will and as you know'; 'The tree of life is high and humility climbs it.' Invoke also the aid of the Holy Spirit: 'Come, Holy Spirit . . . enkindle in me the fire of your love' (See Appendix 2).

It is time, then to confront the state of your heart. We cannot approach the throne of all grace and the presence of unutterable holiness unless we have renounced sin and our attachment to it. Admittedly, this will be part of the combat, because our attachment to sin, which we call concupiscence, does not desert us until the hour of our death. We need to have that resolute determination to leave behind us the burden of our sins. Otherwise the battle is lost before it has begun.

Repentance

We need to own up to our basic unworthiness in the sight of our All-Holy God. This is not an invitation to take on the mantle of Uriah Heep but instead to admit our faults in true humility, conscious of the grandeur of our admission, 'Through repentance we regain our true splendour, just as the moon after a period of waning clothes itself once more in its full light.'[3]

But what of the shame of our admission? Modern novelists (think of Graham Greene) have concentrated on the guilt which they claim derives from the confessional.

They fail to emphasize the therapeutic benefits of being able to admit to one's failings and obtain strength to overcome them which Carl Jung noted in his dealings with Catholic patients.[4] William James says, rather mischievously, 'We English-speaking Protestants, in the general self-reliance and unsociability of our nature, seem to find it enough if we take God alone into our confidence.'[5]

But we are not simply admitting our guilt to ourselves, but to our All Merciful God. St John Chrysostom asks,

> Why, pray tell, are you ashamed, why do you blush to tell your sins? Do you tell them to a man, such as might reproach you? Do you confess them to a fellow-servant, such as might make them public? No, you expose your wound to the Lord, to our kinsman, to the Benefactor of mankind, to the Physician.[6]

For Catholics, this involves going to those 'to whom in the providence of the mystery of God, confession is entrusted'.*

It is not morbid to confront our evil inclinations anymore than it is morbid to confront an infected tooth. The removal of the underlying cause in either case grants us deliverance and freedom. To be attached to God who loves us, we must be detached from all that draws us away from him.

Detachment

It was this spirit of detachment that Jesus held out to the rich young man, 'If you would be perfect, go, sell what you possess and give to the poor, and you will have

---

* St Basil, *Rules Briefly Treated* 288 MG 31.1284.

treasure in heaven; and come, follow me'(Matt 19:21). For the treasure of prayer, we must disencumber ourselves. True prayer is not possible with comfort and indulgence, 'when your soul is attached to the world and to the flesh through desire'.[7] Metropolitan Theoleptos also observes,

> Train yourself for discomfort by reducing comfort little by little, that you may both weaken the strength of the flesh and fortify the soul. For the vanquishing of the flesh secures the victory of the soul and the reasonable distress of the body can bring forth an outpouring of joy for the spirit.[8]

Theoleptos talks of *reasonable* distress because there is always a temptation to go too far. But some mortification should be envisaged. We have to overcome that underlying Anglo-Saxon attitude which was pungently expressed by Mrs John Ruskin when she wrote with obvious horror about 'miracles, the gift of the Spirit, penance and crucifying the flesh'.[9] Those same Victorians would think nothing of punishing ordeals in pursuit of discoveries or commerce but were taught to disparage any spiritual constraint.

Christian writers are almost unanimous in warning against excessive mortification because it can cause irreparable harm and also in a perverse way cater to our baser instincts. The mortification which our modern age needs is rather a resolution to say 'No' from time to time when we are inclined to say 'Yes'. G. K. Chesterton said, on this point, 'We should thank God for his gift of wine, by not drinking too much ...' It is not the thing denied but rather, our unruly *desires*. The *Catechism of the Catholic Church* says that fasting and abstinence 'enables us to obtain mastery over our instincts and freedom of heart'.[10] Any mortification is a means and not an end in itself. Bodily fasting alone is not enough, nor should it be because it must be joined to that circumcision of heart of which St Paul speaks (Rom 2:29) if we are to set aside envy, rancour, malice, insensitivity and avarice which are vices of the soul.[11] Then, we can say that fasting is the soul of prayer, but mercy is the lifeblood of fasting.[12]

Distractions

Part of the combat of prayer is the struggle with distractions. On one occasion, Archbishop Ramsey was asked how long he spent in prayer and he answered, 'about five minutes'. What he meant was that all the rest of the time he spent in prayer was taken up with distractions. But just because we are going to have distractions does not mean that our prayer has any less value. Prayer is that 'interior striving'[13] and that opens us to distractions of every sort. Cassian says that this is because our concentration flags 'or worse, because the demons sow their seeds among us'.[14] Distractions are a by-product of human imperfection and during prayer we are at the mercy of our emotions, temptations and what is called *acedia* or weariness of soul and may be combined with indifference and boredom. Evagrius says, 'against this, tears are a powerful antidote'.[15] Tears are seen as that reaction to our own weakness which silently pleads to God. Rather than wrestle with the manifold spiritual viruses, we offer ourselves humbly to God. Evagrius recommends an interesting psychological analysis, 'Divide the soul tearfully into two halves, one of which comforts while the other is comforted.'[16]

But there is another weapon that can be used with great

effectiveness, referred to as 'spear-thrusts' (*quodam modo iaculatas*: ejaculatory prayers) they are short but persistent invocations. The psalms are particularly useful in this respect, for instance, 'I fear no evil, for you are at my side' (Ps 23: 4); and, 'O God, come to my assistance; O Lord, make haste to help me' (Ps 70:2), which was a favourite of Cassian[17] and of Philip Neri.

Another stratagem relies entirely on the power of the sign of the Cross. Unfortunately for many this has become almost an empty gesture. One of the characteristics of St Bernadette which everyone noticed was her particular way of making this sign 'beautifully ... with a sort of majesty'.[18] Through the Cross, our Saviour conquered for us. By making use of the sign of the Cross with reverence and faith we also invoke his power in our weakness. St Nilus tells us,

> If you want to wipe out the bad memories left in the mind and the multifarious attacks of the enemy, then arm yourself speedily with the recollection of our Saviour and with the ardent invocation of his exalted name by day and by night, while sealing yourself often, both on the forehead and on the breast, with the sign of our Lord's Cross. For as often as the name of our Saviour Jesus Christ is pronounced and the seal of the Lord's Cross is placed on the heart and the forehead and the breast, the power of the enemy) is indubitably quelled, and the wicked demons flee trembling from us.[19]

St Augustine says that one of the proofs of God's meekness is the way he puts up with our wandering thoughts.[20] God sees the person behind all the distractions and the desire to pray which persists ... But there needs to be that persistence. St Makarios of Egypt says, 'He who cultivates prayer has to fight with all diligence and watchfulness, all endurance, all struggle of soul and toil of body, so that he does not become sluggish and surrender himself to distraction.'[21] Yes, we will experience all sorts of wandering thoughts but we should gently bring our mind back to the object of our desires and remind ourselves of our own weakness and God's patience with us: 'Lord God, strength of those who hope in you, support us in our prayer: because we are weak and can do nothing without you, give us always the help of your grace.'[22]

Notes

1. *Meditations and Devotions*, pp. 444–5.
2. St Theodorus the Great Ascetic, *A Century of Spiritual Texts*, n. 8.
3. St John of Karpathos, *For the Encouragement of Monks in India who* had written to him, n. 4.
4 St John Chrysostom, *Homilies on Lazarus*, 4, 4, MG 48.1012.
5. Jung, C.G., pp. 34–63.
6. James, W., p. 443.
7. Theoleptos (1250–1322), *Letter 3 to Princess Irene*, p. 79.
8. Theoleptos, *Letter 1 to Princess Irene*, p. 37.
9 *Effie in Venice: Unpublished Letters of Mrs John Ruskin*, p. 330.
10. *Catechism of the Catholic Church*, n. 2043.
11. John of Damascus (657–749), *On the Virtues and the Vices*, Philokalia, vol. 2, p. 335.
12. St Peter Chrysologus (Bishop of Ravenna 400–450), *Homily 43*.
13. Bunge, p. 11.
14. *Conlationes*, 9.36; Augustine, Letter, 130.20.
15. Evagrius, *Ad Virginem*, n. 39.
16. *Prakticos*, n. 28.
17. *Conference 10*.
18. Trochu, *Bernadette*, p. 221.
19. Nilus, *Epistola 3*, PG 79.521.
20. Cardinal Bellarmine, 21 June 1609, Homily at Roman College, quoted in *Brodrick*, vol. 1, p. 311.
21. *On Prayer*, n. 21.
22. *Collect* for Eleventh Sunday of the Year in the Roman Missal.

Chapter 3

The Sources of Prayer

St Benedict says that if anyone wishes to make a private prayer he should simply go into the Oratory of the monastery and pray. He presumes that the diet of the psalms and the readings would provide ample material . . .

And so they should in theory. The problem is most people do not live in the monastic environment and their only contact with it is on Sunday in church. To expect to pray in that situation is almost like expecting your car to start when it has been lying in the garage for weeks. We may try and coax the starter but all we get are a few bronchial sputterings.

The Word of God

If the children of Israel had to gather manna each day, then we must feed ourselves with spiritual manna before we begin to pray. We need spiritual thoughts to enter our minds, 'Reading is the first step, as it were the foundation which provides the material from which one passes on to meditation.'[1] All spiritual writers put the Scriptures in the first place, because they are the word of God 'living and active, sharper than any two-edged sword, piercing to the division of soul and spirit . . . discerning the thoughts and intentions of the heart' (Heb 4:12). St Aelred reflects on the impact of Scripture in a homily on Isaiah,

> I tell you brethren, nothing contrary can happen, nothing sad or bitter occur, which does not either quickly go, or prove more easy to bear as soon as the sacred page explains it to us. This is the field into which the Holy Isaac went forth to meditate [Gen 24:63], the day being now well spent, where Rebecca coming to meet him softened with her gentleness the affliction that was his. How often my good Jesu, the day draws towards evening; how often to the daylight of some little consolation the dark night of some unsupportable sadness succeeds. All is turned to weariness; everything I see, a burden. If someone speaks, I scarcely hear; if someone knocks, I am hardly aware of it. My heart is hardened like a stone, I cannot speak, my eyes are dry. What then? I go forth to meditate in the field; I turn over the Holy Book, and write my thoughts on the tablet, when suddenly thy grace, good Jesu, like Rebecca running up, disperses the darkness with its light, drives away weariness, breaks my hardness.[2]

We must have Aelred's confidence in the efficacy of God's holy word. We must turn to it every day. Louis Bouyer commenting on the evangelical approach to the Scriptures says,

> They want to fix their whole attention on him who speaks in it, to whom they answer now as a child answers his father or mother . . . direct, familiar, heart to heart intercourse with God, created, upheld, ceaselessly renewed by individual reading of the Bible, with prayer to God which is felt, above all, in a response to his own Word . . . Reading the Bible in the spirit of faith means, strictly speaking, renewing oneself continually in the apprehension of these great truths; for these are not truths of a static kind which man

may take hold of and incorporate into some sort of conceptual system of his own devising. They are truly the shadow cast by the very Truth of God, the God of Jesus Christ, coming down to us.[3]

This recalls the preaching of St Augustine when he invites his congregation, 'Let us listen to the Gospel as though the Lord himself were present. The Lord is above ... but the Lord of truth is here.'[4] Because of its very nature, we must allow ourselves to fall under its influence. We must measure our lives by its truth as Gregory points out, 'Holy Scripture is set before our minds like a mirror, that we may see our inward face in it. It is there that we come to know our ugliness and our beauty. There we realize what progress we are making, how far we are from improvement.'[5] This constant reflection on the Scriptures will permeate our minds, filling them with our other home which God has prepared for those who love him,

> If we always return to our reflections on Holy Scripture and go back to the memory of spiritual things, the desire for what is perfect and the hope of future happiness, it will be inevitable that this will give rise to spiritual thoughts which will keep our minds occupied with what we have been thinking.[6]

Maybe we have a reading guide which provides a section of the Old Testament and of the New for each day, or we can consult the readings for the daily Liturgy of the Word. Admittedly we need to read Scripture with reverence.

This means that we must accept it as Revelation. But at the same time, there is a dual danger that we cling to literalism or we regard Scripture as poetry. Augustine wrote:

> It is a complete mistake to suppose that no narrative of events in this type of literature has any significance beyond the purely historical record, but it is equally rash to hold that every single statement in these books is a complex of allegorical meanings.[7]

Newman pointed out that literalism was the downfall of the school of Antioch which became 'the very metropolis of heresy'.[8]

On the other hand, the Alexandrian school which opted for a more spiritual sense, remained orthodox. This spiritual sense needs to be born in mind when we read because it will deepen our understanding and our reverence. In case we think we are somehow undermining the word of God, Pius XII wrote in 1943, 'Let Catholic exegetes then disclose and expound this spiritual significance, intended and ordained by God, with that care which the dignity of the divine word demands.'[9] The Pope warned against taking things too far, but he would have had in mind the thought-processes of someone like Origen who commented wryly on Abraham's impending sacrifice of his son:

> [Abraham] lifted up his eyes and looked, and behold, behind him was a ram, caught in the thicket by his horns. We have already said, I think, that Isaac was a type of Christ, but here the ram also seems equally to prefigure him. It is worthwhile making the effort to discover how Isaac who was spared and the ram who was slain could both equally represent Christ.[10]

Augustine used the same method when he quoted Christ

saying, 'Do not cling to me, because I have not ascended to my Father' (John 20:17). He goes on,

> What does cling then mean except to believe? For by faith, we cling, we hold on to Christ ... If you suppose Christ to have been but a man, you have held on to him on earth. If you believe Christ to be God, equal to the Father, then you hold on to him when he has ascended to the Father.[11]

Such a grasp of the spiritual sense of Scripture which was so much a part of early Christianity will enrich our reading of Scripture, preventing it from becoming somewhat of a perusal of a series of literary masterpieces (which it is). Our reading should allow us to get to the heart of God's word and in the process allow our hearts to burn within us as the Scriptures are opened to us (cf. Luke 24:32). Kallistos Ware remarks,

> Approached in a prayerful manner, the Bible is found to be always contemporary – not just writings composed in the distant past but a message addressed directly to me here and now. 'He who is humble in his thoughts and engaged in spiritual work' says St Mark the Monk 'when he reads the Holy Scriptures will apply everything to himself and not to someone else.' As a book uniquely inspired by God and addressed to each of the faithful personally, the Bible possesses sacramental power, transmitting grace to the reader, bringing him to a point of meeting and decisive encounter.[12]

Praying with a book ...

We need to take up the words of Scripture, reading them slowly and reflectively, such is *lectio divina* (cf. Chapter 6). As we allow the words to sink into our mind we ask the Holy Spirit to prompt in us the response of a Samuel, who said, 'Speak Lord, your servant is listening' (1 Sam 3:9).

St Teresa of Avila tells us,

> During all these [eighteen] years, except after communicating, I never dared begin to pray without a book; my soul was as much afraid to engage in prayer without one as if it were having to go and fight against a host of enemies. With this help, which was a companionship to me and a shield with which I could parry the blows of my many thoughts, I felt comforted.[13]

As we read we should not rush to get to the end of the chapter, but pause from time to time to allow for prayer to arise in our hearts. *The Imitation of Christ* tells us, 'Read so as to soften the heart, not so as to divert the mind.'[14] St Francis de Sales tells us that 'I have sought rest everywhere, and have found it nowhere save in a little corner with a little book ... Spiritual reading is "the oil of the lamp of prayer".'[15] He was of the opinion that one should not flit from book to book but choose one and 'read it much and practise its teaching'.[16] But such reading must not be rushed. De Caussade advises, 'Pause briefly, from time to time, to let these pleasant thoughts sink deeper into your soul, and allow the Holy Spirit to work. During these peaceful pauses and quiet waiting, he will engrave these heavenly truths upon your heart.'[17]

The Passion of Christ

One specific object of our prayer which was favoured above all by the saints was the Passion of Christ. The Stations of the Cross reenact the journey which pilgrims made in Jerusalem from Pilate's judgement seat to the tomb, using fourteen points for meditation around the walls of churches. The sorrowful mysteries of the rosary do the same. St Ignatius devotes the third week of his *Exercises* to the events of the Passion. Archbishop Goodier's *The Passion and Death of Our Lord Jesus Christ* ran to ten editions between 1933 and 1965. St Francis de Sales explains why it should be so important,

> Christ on the Cross is the Lion of the tribe of Judah and the best interpretation of Samson's riddle – 'out of the strong came forth sweetness' (Jdg. 14:14). In his wounds we find the honeycomb of true love, and from this strength issues forth our best consolation. Indeed as the death of our Lord was the crowning act of his love for us, so might it become the most powerful motive which incites our love for him.[18]

The lives of the saints

St Francis de Sales also recommended reading the lives of the saints which he called 'The Gospel carried into practice.'[19] It was a crucial stage in the life of St Ignatius. When he lay wounded after the siege of Pamplona he exhausted the stock of romances and turned to the lives of the saints. He was fired by their zeal, 'Supposing I were to do what St Francis and St Dominic have done? The example of the saints are given to us as an encouragement above all to provide a certain energy to our prayer so that it leads to action in our own lives.

The *Our Father*

In second place must come the prayer of all prayers, the *Our Father,* called 'the summary of the whole Gospel'.[20] It is the fundamental Christian prayer because this is the Son of God himself telling us. Moreover, it is not simply *a* prayer, but the pattern for prayer itself.

We dare to say *Father* and we adore and glorify the God who made all things and who made us to know him, love him and serve him, and to be happy with him forever in heaven. Surely the very thought of our loving Father is 'learning enough even to my life's end' as St John Fisher said when he took up his bible on his way to execution.[21]

We ask our Father to give us each day that Bread of Life which truly sanctifies us and to bring us to forgive those who hate and persecute us as did Jesus forgive his executioners. We beg him for the grace not to fall into sin and so separate ourselves from his love. All the ingredients of prayer are there: adoration, thanksgiving, sorrow, and petition.

Other prayers

We can also use other prayers, in particular, The Creed, The Doxology: Glory be to the Father, and to the Son, and to the Holy Spirit, and the Hail Mary. We can also pray The Magnificat (Luke 1:46-56), The Benedictus (Luke 1:68-80) and the Nunc Dimittis (Luke 1:29-33) which form part of the Liturgy of the Hours.

The rosary

The rosary has been rightly called 'an epitome of the whole Gospel'.[22] It was promoted by the Cistercians and Dominicans as an alternative to the recitation of the one hundred and fifty psalms in monasteries, in other words, 'a popular substitute for the Liturgy of the Hours'.[23] It has hidden depths because

> In the rosary we can contemplate the mystery of Christ at many levels, from the childlike words of trust and confidence contained in the prayers themselves, through meditation on the mysteries of our Lord's loving work for us, to the heights of mystical union with the mind and heart of Christ.[24]

Pope John Paul II rather courageously added the luminous mysteries* to the devotion of the three joyful, sorrowful and glorious mysteries. The repetition of Our Father and Hail Mary forms the background in the mind for meditation on the individual mystery, rather like *sutras* in Buddhism. Tibetan Buddhist use a *mala* (garland) of one hundred and eight beads to recite mantras. In the same way, Muslims use ninety-nine beads (*misbaha*) corresponding to the names of Allah. It has been remarked that the very 'monotony' of the practice is 'a way of restricting reflective consciousness. If things become too interesting at the rational discursive level, one may want to stay there; one may cling to one's interesting thought, losing the desire to break through to something deeper. If, on the other hand, monotony predominates at the discursive level, the intuitive is allowed to act'.[25]

---

* The Baptism in the Jordan, Marriage Feast at Cana, Proclamation of the Kingdom, The Transfiguration and The Last Supper.

The Eucharist

All of this presumes that there is that daily recourse to the Eucharist. Christ is the life of the Church and the life of each individual which we term members of his mystical body. We are called to live by means of his life. The fourteenth-century mystical writer, Nicolas Cabasilas points out,

> Since it was not possible for us to ascend and participate in that which is his, he comes down to us and participates in that which is ours. And so precisely does he conform to the things which he assumed that, in giving those things to us which he has received from us, he gives himself to us. Partaking of the body and blood of his humanity, we receive God himself into our souls.[26]

St Athanasius summarizes, 'We are made as gods by the flesh of Christ.'[27] That is not to say that we become divine but there is a real union with Christ's deifying grace. The Eastern Fathers emphasize that 'The human race was redeemed by the very fact that the Word united to himself a human nature and we were all affected by the entry of God into our midst.'[28] Through his divinizing flesh hidden beyond the veil of the appearances of bread and wine (as his humanity while on earth veiled his divinity), we gain a share in his eternal and incorruptible life.[29]

But there is also a social dimension in the sense that 'All who eat Christ's holy flesh enter into bodily union with him, and not only with him who is in us through his flesh, but with each other.'[30] By our sharing in the Eucharist we are given a strong sense of the communion of saints and the living reality of the Church which unites all the members together. The Eucharist introduces us into that communion which reaches beyond earth and is a constant reminder of our eternal homeland.

Additional helps

When we are reading and a particular passage strikes us, it is a good idea to remember it and either put it on an index card or in your notebook or your computer database so that it is not lost. It will be a source of inspiration for your prayer and to remind you of those spiritual oases when 'dryness' comes. The same applies to the book itself. If you found it of use, make it part of your library, underline passages which you find useful. Spiritual illiteracy is as harmful as its secular equivalent. There are also the numerous compositions which the saints used to formulate their own prayers. From time to time you may find them useful.[31]

The next two chapters examine the witness to prayer firstly, in the early centuries. We notice a renewed understanding of prayer in the fourteenth (with the *Devotio Moderna*) and then in the sixteenth and seventeenth centuries (which partly explains the emergence of so many new religious Orders). In the more recent past there have also been numerous spiritual writers and I have selected a sample of those who offer their own special insights into the journey of prayer.

Notes
1. Guigo II, *The Carthusian*, chapter 11, ML 184.476.
2. Homily 14, *On the Burden of Isaiah*, quoted in Squire, *Aelred of Rievaulx*, p. 144.
3. Bouyer, p. 12.

The Sources of Prayer 27

4. *In Joan. Tract. 30, 1*, PL 35, 1632.
5. *Moralia in Job, 2, 1* PL 75, 353.
6. John Cassian (360–435), *Conlationes 1.18*, PL 49, 50.
7. Augustine, *City of God*, Book 17, chapter 3.
8. *An Essay on The Development of Christian Doctrine*, p. 343.
9. Chinigo, p. 277 (from the Encyclical *Divino Afflante Spiritu*, n. 26; cf. also Pontifical Biblical Commission 1983) nn 129–43.
10. *On Genesis*, 8, 8.
11. *Sermon 246*, nn 4, 5.
12. Ware, *The Orthodox Way*, p. 149.
13. *Life*, chapter 4.
14. Book 1, chapter 20.
15. Camus, pp. 54, 55.
16. Ibid; *Introduction to the Devout Life*, Book 2, 17.
17. De Caussade, *Letter* 111 *to the Visitandine nuns at Nancy*.
18. Camus, p. 54.
19. Camus, p. 55.
20. Tertullian, *On Prayer*, n. 1, PL1, 1255.
21. Macklem, p. 205. The quotation is from John 17:3.
22. *Catechism of the Catholic Church*, 971.
23. Ibid, 2678.
24. Anon. in *Faith*, 40, 4 July 2008, p. 22.
25. William Johnston, p. 59.
26. *De Vita in Christo*, 4,9, PL 150, 593.
27. *Adversus Ariannos*, *3, 24*, MG 26, 373.
28. O'Neill, p. 190.
29. Mantzaridis, pp. 53–41.
30. Cf. Lercaro, pp. 300–5.
31. Maximos the Confessor (580–662), *Hermeneia on Prayer*, PG 90, 877.

Chapter 4

The Saints and Spiritual Writers – 1

> Come, let us look at those warriors who conquered, who excelled in both faith and prayer.
> Ephrem the Syrian, *Armenian Prayer*

We need first to listen to that 'living and abiding voice' which is the witness of the early writers, the Fathers of the Church,[1] on their experience of prayer.

The apostolic age

The *Didache* notes, in passing, Jesus' words about hypocrisy in prayer and fasting and goes on to recommend the *Our Father*. It adds, 'Pray thus three times a day.'[2] St Peter went up to the housetop to pray about the sixth hour, when he had his vision (Acts 10:9ff). We can deduce that the early Church remained generally faithful to Jewish prayer practice, while making certain adaptations. A modern Rabbi has written that the present *Siddur*' or prayer book, 'has been the gate to communion with their Father in heaven'.[3] There is no reason to question whether the Christian community would have drawn on their Jewish heritage to turn to their Lord and God, with even greater love, since those who had seen Jesus had truly seen the Father also (John 14:9).

We can see this in *The Martyrdom* of St Polycarp (69–155), a disciple of St John the Evangelist. As he was about to die in the amphitheatre at Smyrna, we are told that he looked up to heaven and prayed, 'For all things do I praise you, I do bless you. I do glorify you through the eternal and heavenly High Priest, Jesus Christ, your beloved Child: through whom be glory to you with Him and the Holy Spirit, both now and through ages yet to come. Amen.'[4] It is precisely because we have such a High Priest that Christians are urged to 'give glory to Him who redeemed them from death' and 'not to come to prayer with a bad conscience'.[5]

This point is taken up by St Justin, the philosopher, in his defence of Christianity addressed to the Emperor Antonius Pius concerning the Sacrament of baptism: 'Whoever is convinced and believes that what they are taught and told by us is the truth, and professes to be able to live accordingly, is instructed to pray and to beseech God in fasting for the remission of their former sins, while we pray and fast with them.'[6] This echoes the words in the Letter of St James,

> Is any among you sick? Let them call for the elders of the church, and let them pray over him, anointing him with oil in the name of the Lord; and *the prayer of faith* will save the sick man, and the Lord will raise him up; and if he has committed sins, he will be forgiven. (Jas 5:14–16)

Thus prayer is seen to be intimately connected with the Liturgy from the very beginning.

The Eastern Fathers

Out of their desert experience came the concept of the soul's battle against the demons both within and without. We, who have dismissed the idea of demonic activity, tend also to reject the concept of temptation and the desire for unspeakable evil. In that wilderness of heat and loneliness the Desert Fathers faced up to their demons. St Mark the Ascetic compares these inner demons to three giants of the Philistines,

> These three giants are ignorance, the source of all evils, forgetfulness, its close relation and helper; and laziness, which weaves the dark shroud enveloping the soul in murk. This third vice supports and strengthens the other two, consolidating them so that evil becomes deep-rooted and persistent in the negligent soul. Laziness, forgetfulness, and ignorance in their turn support and strengthen the other passions.[7]

St Anthony the Great observes that the soul's senses are attacked through the five bodily senses, 'Through these five senses the unhappy soul is taken captive when it succumbs to its four passions. These four passions are self-esteem, levity, anger, and cowardice.'[8] Fasting is part of the armour which we need to undertake the campaign of prayer. St Isaiah says, 'When the intellect grows strong, it makes ready to pursue the love that quenches all bodily passions and that prevents anything contrary to nature from gaining control over the heart.'[9] Because the writers were mostly male and monks, we might suppose that they would be introspective and clinical in their approach but instead we find that they display a great balance and objectivity and this explains their continuing popularity in the collection known as the

Philokalia which was edited in the eighteenth century by Nikodimos of Mount Athos and Makarios of Corinth.

They also took literally St Paul's injuction to pray constantly. (1 Thess 5:7) Origen in turn notes, 'Those who give themselves continually to prayer know by experience that through this frequent practice they avoid innumerable sins and are led to perform many good deeds.'[10] St Anthony the Great told his followers, 'Breathe Christ at all times, and believe in him.'[11] The great Barsanuphios pronounced that it was not necessary to prolong the actual words 'for throughout the entire day your intellect is at prayer'.[12] But the spiritual life echoed with the impact of Scripture, in particular the Psalms (which eventually became the Liturgy of the Hours). They were like the tolling of the bells, recalling the soul to God, 'When you sit down to your handiwork, you should learn by heart or recite psalms. At the end of each psalm you should pray sitting: "O God, have mercy on me, a miserable man." When you are troubled by thoughts, then add, "O God, see my affliction, come to my aid."'[13] We can see here the origin of the *Jesus Prayer*[14] and of similar short invocations, or 'spear thrusts' so popular in Orthodoxy. All express humble confidence in the almighty power of God, to come to the assistance of the sinful soul, 'O God, be gracious to me, a sinner', 'Lord, help me', 'Son of God, have mercy on me', 'Lord, save me from the evil one.'[15] These gradually migrate to Western Christianity in the form of aspirations 'to keep the flame of faith alight'.

The power of fasting

Prayer is also joined with fasting. It is interesting that the same modern revulsion towards abstinence of any kind extends to fasting but doctors frequently recommend its use to patients in the interests of their health. The early Christian Fathers did not see fasting as an end in itself and frequently spoke out against the danger of hypocrisy, quoting the words of Jesus (Matt. 6:16-18). Someone was asked, 'How do I find God?' the answer of the Fathers was, 'by fasting, by watching, by labours, by mercy, and, above all these, by discernment. For I say to you, many have tormented the flesh without discernment and have gone away empty, without getting anything for it'.[16]

The ultimate reason for fasting which always needs to be kept in mind, is humility. We know that God 'humbled' the children of Israel in the wilderness, letting them go hungry (Deut 8:3). In fact, 'Nothing humbles the soul, as does fasting.'[17] Over-indulgence on the other hand exposes us to shameful desires and irrational anger, as in the case of Noah when he was drunk (Gen 9:21). Evagrius observes trenchantly, 'A famished stomach enables one to watch in prayer, whereas a full stomach brings about plentiful sleep.'[18]

It is recorded that when a neighbouring parish priest complained to St John Vianney, the Curé of Ars, that his parishioners were irreligious, he replied, 'Have you fasted for them?'[19] The early Fathers were not so immersed in mystical contemplation that they disregarded the need to take the body with them with all its weaknesses, in their ascent of the holy mountain of prayer.

Into the darkness

The Eastern Fathers talk of *dispassion* or the absence of unruly passions, as a state to be aimed at; what Hesychius of Sinai refers to as 'an undisturbed tranquility'.[20] We tend to assume that we can dive into prayer and then find that it is difficult to settle our mind on spiritual things. St Neilos observes,

> Those who have only recently escaped from the agitation of the world should be advised to practice stillness; otherwise, by frequently going out, they will reopen the wounds inflicted on their mind through the senses. They should take care not to add new images to their old fantasies. Those who have only just renounced the world find stillness hard to practice, for memory now has time to stir up all the filth that is within then, whereas previously it had no chance to do this because of their many preoccupations ... they should keep their intelligence in a state of profound calm, far from all that irritates it.[21]

Even if we bear in mind that this is written for those who forsake the world to live a solitary life, it surely applies to all who wish to set out on the spiritual path. St Thalassios is adamant that 'The forceful practice of self-control and love, patience and stillness, will destroy the passions hidden within us.'[22]

In a similar way they talk of the eradication of all images and positive knowledge in order to attain the Absolute Unknowable that is God, 'for man shall not see me and live' (Exo 33:20). This *apophatic* (= by way of denial) approach 'is an ascendant understanding of the mind that progressively eliminates all positive attributes of the object it wishes to attain, in order to culminate finally in a kind of apprehension by supreme ignorance of Him who cannot be an object of knowledge'.[23] Certainly this tends to run counter to the Western tendency to proceed systematically from stage to stage until a conclusion is reached. However, as we shall see, St John of the Cross makes a strong case for this approach.

In the image of God ...

Just as fasting is not an end in itself, so also we are not supposed to cast anchor in stillness and the apophatic approach. The aim should be a recovery of that image and likeness to God in which we are made (Gen 1:27). The Letter to the Colossians reminds us 'that we have put on the new nature, which is being renewed in knowledge after the image (*eikon*) of its creator' (Col 3:10). St Maximos the Confessor observes,

> If we are made, as we are, in the image of God ... let us all become the image of the one whole God, bearing nothing earthly in ourselves, so that we may consort with God and become gods, receiving from God our existence as gods ... God made us so that we might become 'partakers of the divine nature' (2 Pet 1:4) and sharers in his eternity, and so that we might come to be like him through deification by grace.[24]

We might think this is too presumptive but grace and our rebirth in the Spirit does raise us up to the dignity of communion with God, above our own nature, so that we can share the divine life. St Gregory Palamas calls grace 'the resplendence and deifying energy of God which deifies those who participate in it'.[25] Have we set our sights too low? Maximos is unrepentant when he says 'God who yearns for the salvation of all and hungers for their deification, withers their conceit like the unfruitful fig tree' (Matt 21:19-21).[26] If we take seriously the impact on created humanity of the Incarnation, then we must want to experience fully its effects. St Symeon says,

> Surely it is that Christ has shared in what is ours so as to make us participants in what he is. For the Son of God

became the Son of man in order to make us human beings sons of God, raising us up by grace to what he is by nature, giving us a new birth in the Holy Spirit and leading us directly into the kingdom of heaven. Or, rather, he gives us the grace to possess this kingdom within ourselves, so that not merely do we hope to enter it, but being in full possession of it, we can affirm: 'Our life is hid with Christ in God.' (Col 3:3)[27]

Voices from the West

As in the East, the first witness to the essential elements of prayer came from monasticism. St Benedict has already been mentioned, but before Benedict was St John Cassian (or Cassyon) c.360–435. He joined a monastery in Bethlehem and later studied in Egypt but is known for his two foundations in the West near Marseilles where he wrote his two books, *Institutes* and *Conferences*. He brought to the West many of the Eastern traits which we have already discussed, such as the need for humility, renunciation, stillness and prayer which rises above human consciousness 'with no voice sounding, no tongue moving, no words uttered'.[28] But he also examines the psychology of the person who desires to pray and points out that an equilibrium needs to be achieved. He writes,

> In advance of prayer we must strive to dispose ourselves as we would wish to be during prayer. For the mind in prayer is shaped by the state that it was previously in, and, when we sink into prayer, the image of the same deeds, words, and thoughts plays itself out before our eyes. This makes us angry or sad, depending on our previous condition, or it recalls past lusts or business, or it strikes us with foolish laughter ... First, anxiety about fleshly matters should be completely cut off. Then, not only the concern for but in

> fact even the memory of affairs and business should be refused all entry whatsoever: detraction, idle speech, talkativeness, and buffoonery – all such like must be cut out. The disturbance of anger, in particular, and of gloominess should also be eradicated.[29]

He argues also that our character will have an influence on the way we pray, not simply in proportion to the degree of purity in the soul,

> A lively person prays one way. A person brought down by the weight of gloom or despair prays another. One prays another way when pushed down by the mass of temptation. One prays differently depending on whether one is seeking the gift of some grace or virtue, of the removal of some sinful vice.[30]

He is also the first to make a fourfold division of prayer (which differs slightly from our modern classification) into supplications, prayers, intercessions, and thanksgiving, basing himself on the Letter to Timothy (1 Tim 2:1). He describes a supplication as 'a petition concerning sins, by which a person begs for pardon for his present or past misdeeds'. Prayers are 'those acts by which we offer or vow something to God'. Intercessions are 'on behalf of our dear ones and for the peace of the whole world'. Thanksgivings recall 'God's past benefits, contemplate his present ones or foresee what he has prepared for those who love him'.[31] He sees the *Our Father* as containing 'the utter fullness of perfection' not simply because of its author but also because it lifts up those who use it 'to that prayer of fire known to so few. It lifts these up to that ineffable prayer which rises about all human consciousness'.[32]

On distractions in prayer he does not dismiss the idea

of external 'incursions' but he argues strongly in favour of the power of the individual strengthened by grace,

> It is not possible that the mind should be impervious to thoughts. But these must not be attributed completely either to some incursion or those spirits which strive to slip them in among us. Otherwise man's free will would not remain nor would our task of self-discipline continue to be there. But I would say that to a great extent it is up to us to ensure the good character of our thoughts. It depends on us whether they turn holy and spiritual or else earthly or of the flesh.[33]

Cassian also makes the point that going into our inner room and shutting the door 'we offer our petitions to the one who pays no attention to words but looks hard at our hearts'.[34]

Augustine (354–430)

It is not unexpected that one of the most celebrated and influential saints in Western Christianity, whose writings fill volumes, should also have spoken about prayer. Augustine's life (such as he has told to us in his *Confessions*) combined activity and contemplation. He was a bishop in North Africa and also the founder of a monastery. He battled the heterodox opinions of his day and yet he spent time guiding people like Faltonia Proba, the virgin Sapida and Valerius in the ways of the spiritual life.

Augustine experienced for himself the love of God which brought him to Christianity and he was convinced that our hearts are restless until they rest in God,

> Let your longing be known to Him, our Father, and he, who sees hidden things, will reward you. For it is your heart's desire that is your prayer and if your desire endures, then

your prayer too shall endure ... If you wish to pray without end, then keep the desire of your heart alive. The continuation of your longing is the continuation of your prayer. If you no longer love, then your prayer, too, will end.[35]

Prayer implies for Augustine the gift of oneself, not some attitude or gesture. We offer to God our very life, 'The victim to sacrifice is within myself; the incense to place upon the altar is within me; the sacrifice to offer to my God is within.'[36] In another place he says,

> Now the psalmist freely loved God, willingly sacrificed to him, and leaving behind the things of earth, he saw nothing else in the heights on which to pour out his spirit except God, from whom, through whom and in whom he had been created, and to whom he had turned, saying; 'My voice goes up to God.'[37]

So in his Rule, which he wrote around 397, he can say, 'When you pray to God in psalms and song, the words spoken by your lips should also be alive in your hearts.'[38]

This awareness of God's love for us, and our need to respond, flowed out of a profound experience which will be repeated in the lives of many saints when he records that mystical experience in his life,

> It was higher because it created me, and I was lower because I was something made. He who knows the truth knows that light, and he who knows it knows eternity. Love knows it. O Eternal Truth and True Love and Beloved Eternity! You are my God, to you I sigh day and night ... And I found myself to be far from you in the land of unlikeness, as I heard your voice from on high: 'I am the food of the strong. Grow and you will eat of me. And you will not change me into yourself, like the food of your flesh; but you will be changed into me.'[39]

When we set out on the road to pray we cannot know where the journey will lead – God knows. Augustine opens to us that horizon which the mystics experience but which is not for all, so that we can have some of that spirit of wonder and praise in our own prayer.

The *Devotio Moderna*

The movement called 'Modern Devotion' spread from Holland to parts of Germany, France and Italy at the end of the fourteenth century. It included Jan van Ruysbroeck, Thomas a Kempis and John Tauler.

Thomas a Kempis, who was born in Kempen in 1379, became sub-prior of the Augustinian monastery at Mount St Agnes near Zwolle in 1425. He wrote *The Imitation of Christ* probably between 1420 and 1427. Although written primarily for monks, it gained an ever increasing lay readership and was a favourite with John Wesley and Daniel O'Connell. In its almost intimate style it urges the reader to greater holiness,

> If you can't be in a state of recollection all the time, at least you should collect your thoughts at intervals; at the very least once a day, every morning, let us say, or every evening. Morning is the time for making resolutions; when evening comes, analyse your past behaviour – what sort of person have you been today? What have you said, or done; what have been your thoughts?[40]

At the heart of prayer he places the love of Jesus,

> Up with you then, faithful soul, get your heart ready for the coming of this true Lover, or he will never consent to come and make his dwelling in you ... Be pure and free of heart; don't let yourself get wrapped up in anything created. You

must strip yourself bare and bring God a pure heart if you wish to be free to see how sweet the Lord is.[41]

Thomas gently argues for a resolute following of Christ who bore his Cross for us, renouncing all that prevents us from listening to 'the soft whisper of God's voice'.

> Let not Moses speak to me, but you, my Lord and my God, you the eternal Truth; otherwise I may die and bear no fruit, if I have been warmed only from outside and not been kindled to flame within ... When you come into my heart, the whole of my inmost being will leap with joy.[42]

John Tauler (1300–1361), born at Strasbourg, was a famous Dominican preacher at the time of the Black Death. Prayer is not simply the ascent of the mind to God, it is also the action of God on us,

> The soul must go out. It must travel away from itself, above itself. That is to say that we must deny ourselves our own will and all desire and activity of our own. There must be nothing left in us but a pure intention toward God; no will to be or become or obtain anything for ourselves. We must exist only to make a place for him, the highest innermost place, where he may do His work; there, when we are no longer putting ourselves in His way, he can be born in us.[43]

We can understand the reservations of ecclesiastical superiors with regard to the *Devotio Moderna* because it seems to undermine accepted attitudes. Tauler would seem to be saying that the individual could give lip service to the rule, and fulfilling what Holy Church obliged, while all the time engaging in interior prayer.

> [Such a person] ought to say his prayers and at the same time not say them, he should recollect himself, retreat into

the depths of his soul, raise his heart and direct his faculties to God, inwardly contemplating the presence of God and ardently longing above all things for whatever is dearest to his will. He should withdraw himself from himself and all created things, and sink himself deeper and deeper in God's manifest will. And then he ought to draw into this prayer everything which he has been ordered to do, desiring that his prayer may be for the honour and glory of God and the profit and consolation of those for whom he is bound to pray ... For the Father desires that one pray to him in this way, and all other kinds of prayer serve this kind; and if they don't, simply let them go ... When you come to the great feast of the conversion of your interior life to God, omit any external practices which hinder it, because your interior life is a divine life, filled with joy ... Prayer which is prayed in the spirit is infinitely superior to all external prayer.[44]

Tauler urges people to live a life 'in which activity and joyful contemplation of God form one single whole [and] people who neglect this noble work and let their noble faculties lie idle live terrible and shameful lives, which bring sorrow here on earth'.[45] One can almost hear the mutterings of religious superiors down the ages to such apparently subversive language.

The Cloud of Unknowing

Dom David Knowles described the author of *The Cloud of Unknowing* as having a claim to be 'the most original spiritual writer in the English language'.[46] It was written at the end of the fourteenth century and has been ascribed to Walter Hilton among others. Straightaway we see the connection with other writings of the *Devotio Moderna* when we read, 'Lift up your heart to God with humble love: and mean God himself, and not what you get out of him. Indeed hate to think of anything but God himself, so that nothing occupies your mind or will but only God.[47] Between the soul and God there is this impenetrable cloud but the author urges us to use 'that sharp dart of longing love, this blind outreaching of love' to beat away at it.[48] We will see this developed by St John of the Cross.

Two saints from Spain

St Teresa (1515-1582) and St John of the Cross (1542-1591) were almost exact contemporaries in life and in works. Both were instrumental in the reform of the Carmelite Order. For a time St John was the spiritual director of St Teresa. They were obviously kindred spirits.

St Teresa managed to combine great common sense and deep spirituality. She also had the ability to express this in her writings. When it came to describe prayer she made use of an image familiar to Castile,

> It seems to me that the garden can be watered in four ways: by taking the water from a well, which costs us great labour; or by a water wheel and buckets, when the water is drawn by a windlass (I have sometimes drawn it in this way: it is less laborious than the other and gives more water); or by a stream or a brook, which waters the ground much better, for it saturates it more thoroughly and there is less need to water it often, so that the gardener's labour is much less; or by heavy rain, when the Lord waters it with no labour of ours, a way incomparably better than any of those which have been described ... It has seemed possible to me in this way to explain something about the four degrees of prayer to which the Lord, of his goodness, has occasionally brought my soul.[49]

St Teresa had a great gift to explain the paths of prayer in such a graphic way. Beginners on the journey of prayer find the going hard,

> At first it causes distress, for beginners are not always sure that they have repented of their sins ...Then they have to endeavour to meditate upon the life of Christ and this fatigues their minds ... Our task is to draw up water from the well and do what we can to water the flowers.[50]

But supposing the well is dry? Teresa deals with aridity in prayer also.

> God keeps the flowers alive without water and makes the virtues grow. The gardener [us] will be glad and take heart and consider it the greatest of favours to work in the garden of so great an Emperor; and, as he knows that he is pleasing him by so working (and his purpose must be to please, not himself, but him), let him render him great praise for having placed such confidence in him, when he has seen that, without receiving any recompense, he is taking such great care of that which he had entrusted to him; let him help him to bear the Cross and consider how he lived with it all his life long; let him not wish to have kingdom on earth or ever cease from prayer, and so let him resolve, even if this aridity should persist his whole life long, never to let Christ fall beneath the Cross. The time will come when he shall receive his whole reward at once.[51]

This experience is not uncommon. St Joan Frances de Chantal, the foundress of the Visitation Order (1572–1641) who has been called 'the saint of prayer', spent the last eight years of her life in periods of aridity and the feeling that God had abandoned her.

The soul which perseveres in prayer, even to the extent of using additional help (Teresa uses a windlass – by water wheel and buckets) will attain to the prayer of quiet. In this state the will is fixed on loving God, while the mind actively helps the will:

> It gives simple consent to become a prisoner of God, for it knows well what it is to be the captive of him it loves; ... the labour is so slight that the prayer is never wearisome. The reason is that the understanding is now working very gradually and it is drawing much more water than it drew out of the well.[52]

In the third state where the garden is watered by a brook it could be said the God almost takes over the work, 'This seems to me to be nothing else but an almost complete death to all the things of this world and an enjoyment of God ... involving a sleep of the faculties and a beginning of ecstasy.'[53]

Teresa explains that she was raised to this state of prayer some five or six years previously and after giving the illustration says that she never understood it nor could explain it fully.

St John of the Cross approaches the same situation from a poetic standpoint of the journey of the soul, 'my house being now at rest'. Whereas Teresa talks of a sleep of the intellect and will, St John talks of the first and second nights. The first night is the purgation of the sensual part of the soul and the second the purgation of the spiritual part.[54]

St John puts the emphasis on the guiding hand of God's love for the soul goes on its journey 'led by God, through love of him only, and with that love inflamed into the dark night'.[55] This darkness is the process by which our wishes and desires are mortified, and finding no pleasure in them 'abide in darkness'.[56] It is also the darkness of faith itself which is like night: obscure and beyond our reasoning. Finally, God is in himself darkness visible, 'as night to the soul'; 'We must pass through these three nights if we are to attain to divine union with God.'[57] St John who wrote this description between 1579 and 1585 had experienced his own physical night in December 1577 when he had been imprisoned by a group of unreformed Carmelites and spent eight months in a cell with no windows, ten feet long by six feet wide. When the night is over, 'the soul is transformed by love'.[58]

Notes

1. Papias, PG 20, 297.
2. 8.1.
3. Rabbi J. H. Hertz, *Daily Prayer Book*, p. ix.
4. 14, 3.
5. Barnabas, n. 19.
6. *First Apology*, n. 61.
7. St Mark the Ascetic, *Letter to Nicholas the Solitary*, 'On those who Think They are Made Righteous by Work', n. 119.
8. Anthony, *On the Character of Men and the Virtuous Life*, n. 79.
9. *On Guarding the Intellect*, n. 9.
10. *Prayer: Exhortation to Martyrdom*, n. 15.
11. *Life*, n. 91.
12. Barsanuphios, *Epistola*, 74, 3.
13. Ibid.
14. Discussed in chapter 5.
15. Ammonius 4; Makarios 19 and *Sayings of the Fathers* quoted in Bunge, p. 117.
16. Ward, p. 111.
17. Evagrius, *In Psalm. 34, 13*.
18. *De Octo Spiritibus Malitiae, 1.12*: PG 79, 1145.
19. Trochu, *Curé of Ars*, p. 313.
20. *Philokalia*, vol. 1, p. 142.
21. St Neilos, *Ascetic Discourse*, 1.
22. *On Love, Self-Control and Life in Accord with the Intellect*, n. 8.
23. Lossky, p. 13.

24. *First Century of Various Texts*, nn 28, 42.
25. *Topics of Natural and Theological Science and On the Moral and Ascetic Life*, n. 93.
26. Maximos, *First Century of Various Texts*, n. 74.
27. *One Hundred and Fifty-Three Practical and Theological Texts*, n. 108.
28. 9, 25.
29. 9, 3.
30. 9, 8.
31. 9, 9.
32. 9, 18.
33. 1, 17
34. 9, 35.
35. *Explanation of Psalm 33*.
36. Ibid., 42.
37. Ibid., 77.
38. *Rule, Community Prayer*, n. 4.
39. *Confessions*, 7, 10.
40. Book 1, chapter 19.
41. Book 2, chapters 1, 8.
42. Book 3, chapters 2, 5.
43. *Sermon 6*, p. 156.
44. *Conference 9*.
45. Ibid.
46. Knowles, *English Mystical Tradition*, p. 67.
47. Ibid., chapter 3.
48. Ibid., chapter 12.
49. *Life*, chapter 11.
50. Ibid.
51. Ibid.
52. *Life*, chapter 14.
53. *Life*, chapter 16.
54. *Ascent of Mount Carmel*, Book 1, chapter 1.
55. Ibid.
56. Chapter 3.
57. Chapter 2.
58. Ibid.

Chapter 5

The Saints and Spiritual Writers – 2

St Teresa of Avila and St John of the Cross only came in contact with the Reformation when they found their view suspected by the Inquisition. Teresa's views on the overwhelming love of those who have achieved the heights of prayer and the justification of the individual through the merits of Christ were subject to scrutiny in 1566. Menéndez y Pelayo maintained that St John was delated to the Holy Office four times and was saved from arrest in 1577.

St Francis de Sales

The reaction to the Reformation can be traced in the spirituality of St Ignatius and St Francis de Sales. St Francis de Sales (1567–1622), who was educated in Paris and became a Senator of Savoy, gave up the prospect of a brilliant career for the priesthood. He published the *Introduction to the Devout Life* in 1609 which became an instant classic. Unlike writings with a monastic emphasis, it was written for people who sought to live a holy life in the world.

In contrast to the clinical and fierce theology of Calvin in Geneva, Francis proposed a gentler way. He recalls the

Spanish saints when he says that 'Prayer opens our mind to the brightness of divine light and our will to the warmth of heavenly love, nothing so purges our mind of ignorance and our will of evil desires.'[1] But, addressing Philothea,* he proposes a *method* to achieve this freedom from even the attraction of sin so as to increase the love of God in us.

His scheme of ten meditations begins with our creation by God and progresses via the Four Last Things to the choice of heaven and the devout life. He is not anxious that those on the journey of prayer should get ahead of themselves or aim too high. At the same time he demands serious effort on our part but with great tenderness and compassion. In Morning Prayer for instance, he says, 'Thank God most lovingly for keeping you alive until this morning, and if during the past night you fell into any sin ask his forgiveness.'[2] On dryness in prayer, he tells Philothea, 'Do not be in the least worried, but say some vocal prayers, tell our Lord about it and admit how unworthy you are; ask him to help you ...'[3] His voice is that of gentle pleading, 'Remember God's presence as often as you can during the day ... saying, "O God, why do I not always look on you as you are always looking on me? Why, when you think so often of me, do I think so seldom of you? O my soul, my true place is in God, and where do I so often find myself?"'[4]

St Ignatius

Ignatius of Loyola (1491–1556), a career soldier who, after being wounded, experienced a spiritual conversion

---

* One who loves God.

and retired to live for a year praying and doing penance in the cave of Manresa near Barcelona 1522-3. Out of this experience came *The Spiritual Exercises*. These offer a more radical approach to the spiritual life than St Francis de Sales because, says Gleason, 'His goal was that of an apostolic spirit of generous service, a life of sanctity penetrated by prayer and supporting and invoking it, rather than a spirituality purely contemplative or mystical in its orientation.'[5] This concept of *service* evokes Ignatius' chivalric and military background (he was the youngest of eleven children from a noble Basque family) who lived in a castle, and had been attached to the Court as a page when he was sixteen). The pageantry of the Court, which was overlaid by the heroism of saints and martyrs together with military discipline, provided the recipe for Ignatian spirituality.

Ignatius envisages thirty days or four 'weeks' of *Spiritual Exercises* (the word itself has military connotations).[6] The first week concentrated on the second half of St Francis de Sales' meditations – consciousness of sinfulness and need to do penance. The second week consists of reflections of the life of Christ up to and including Palm Sunday and the Two Standards set before us, 'Christ our Supreme Captain and Lord – Lucifer, the mortal enemy of our human nature.'[7] We are then asked to contemplate the events of the last week of Jesus' life. The final week considers the Resurrection and Ascension. Each day there are five Exercises which last one hour. St Ignatius adds, 'It is better to spend even more than an hour rather than less; since the enemy frequently tries to have us shorten the hour.'[8]

The Ignatian method of *meditation* is one of the most widely used.[9] St Francis de Sales has a preparation, considerations and resolutions. Ignatius goes further. The preparation is more detailed. We must ask of God, 'the grace that all my intentions, actions and works may be directed purely to the service and praise of His Divine Majesty'. We then must recognize our sinfulness and ask for the grace to amend our life. Ignatius divides and systematizes but we can select two main methods of meditation: the Meditated Prayer and Contemplation of the Mysteries of Christ.

In the Meditated Prayer, we can for example take a vocal prayer, such as the *Our Father*, the Hail Mary, a psalm or a prayer from the Liturgy. We say the first word – 'Father' and we pause 'for so long a time as we find *meanings, comparisons, relish and consolation* in considerations belonging to such a word'.[10] We must linger over the meaning and significance and over the affections aroused in the heart. We will draw relish from this and feel consolation. Then we pass on to the next word. It does not matter if we meditate upon one or several words. Finally we ask God for true amendment of life and conclude with a Colloquy to Jesus and Our Lady. St Francis de Sales would rather express this in terms of gathering 'a bouquet of spiritual thoughts to perfume your whole day'.[11]

When we talk of *A Contemplation of the Mysteries of Christ*, we are still in the early stages of prayer, at the level of meditation, not that of *infused* contemplation. We take for instance the mystery of the Nativity. The first prelude is *historical*. We consider how Mary went from Nazareth to Bethlehem with Joseph, making the journey come alive. The second prelude provides us with *composition of place*. In our mind's eye we see the way from Nazareth, considering the hills and valleys until we come to the cave of the Nativity. In our third prelude we ask our Saviour to know him more intimately so as to love and serve him better.

There has been a tendency to disparage such a comprehensive blueprint for prayer. People argue that it is almost prayer-by-numbers. Ignatius designed his *Exercises* primarily for the members of the Society so that they could live and work 'in the field' if needs be, without the protection of a community, yet sanctified in their apostolate. The methods of meditation which spun off from the *Exercises* were simplifications, with the same basic aim for the individual person fighting his daily battle in the world. For the beginner they do not require mind games. Meditated Prayer provides a point of reference to anchor our mind and so is particularly suitable when we are tired or distracted. It helps us to understand the meaning of familiar prayers and give them a greater 'fragrance'. Meschler sums up by saying that using this method people 'often succeed in making excellent and sound meditations'.[12]

Brother Lawrence

Nicholas Herman Lawrence (1605–1691) had been a soldier, like Ignatius. He entered the Carmelite monastery in Paris in 1649 as a lay brother (Brother Lawrence of the Resurrection) where he was given charge of the kitchen. He wrote his *Maximes spirituelles* in 1692.[13] In his book he develops the idea of the omnipresence of God,

> He had reached the point, he said, where he thought only of God ... and when he had some mundane business to do, he gave no thought to it in advance, but, when it was time for

action, he found in God, as in a clear mirror, what was needful to be done at the present moment ... in accordance with the simplicity of his outlook, he did all for the love of God, giving him due thanks for directing what he did, and doing numberless other things, but all very simply, and in a manner which kept him firm in the loving presence of God ... One could become entangled in acts of penitence and special devotions, leaving love which is the end.[14]

There is the delicate aside, 'This exercise cost me not a little, yet I continued it in spite of all difficulties.' Such habitual awareness of the presence of God harks back to the concept of unceasing prayer and fosters it. It also warms the heart which may tire of too much intellectual work. St Teresa of Lisieux confessed that she found she was unable to meditate on the rosary 'try as I will to put force on myself' but that prayer itself 'like a queen has access at all times to the Royal presence'.[15] Bossuet (1627–1704), who was a contemporary of Brother Lawrence, makes the point,

> The presence of God must not be arid, but full of love. Nothing can so well make any object present to us as love, which clasps it to the very depths of our soul, and recalls its every trait. Can one forget, and not have present to one, anything that one loves?[16]

Fr John Nicholas Grou

Fr Grou, SJ (1731–1803), was a professor at the Jesuit College of La Flèche. He lived as a refugee in England from 1792 until his death. His spiritual works had a wide circulation and the two-volume *L'École de Jésus-Christ* was published posthumously, an extract of which was translated as 'How to Pray' in 1885. Père Grou takes up the concept of continuous prayer. 'What is this prayer?' he asks.

It is true prayer - the only kind that really draws God's attention and gives value to all other kinds of prayer. In other words, it is the prayer of the heart ... As soon as the Holy Spirit begins to pray in a heart, it is his intention to go on praying, and it is our fault if he does not ... It is just as easy, therefore, and as natural to the heart, to pray always as to love always. We can always love God, even without thinking of him or telling him so. All that is necessary is to be determined, not only never to do anything opposed to that love, but, on the contrary, to take every opportunity to prove our love by making acts as grace prompts us.[17]

He then goes to provide an example of a meditation on the *Our Father*, 'Like all true prayer, it is meant for the heart rather than for the mind; and while it is necessary to understand it, it is even more necessary for the heart to respond to it.'[18] He tells us, God is *our* Father, 'The man whom God thinks worthy of his love - do you not think him worthy of yours? And because you do not love him, you think that God should not love him either.'[19] When we say *Hallowed be Thy Name*, 'Think of who God is and what he deserves; what he has done for you, what he promises you and what he expects of you. Can we ever do too much in this respect, where God's glory is concerned?'[20] To say *Thy will be done* is not wishful thinking, 'You may be sure [God] knows our weakness better than we do, but he knows also the power of grace, and what it can accomplish in a heart entirely given over to him.'[21] Père Grou does not make impossible demands, 'I am not asking if we have advanced far on the road, but simply whether we have set out on it. Do we at least wish, and are we trying, to be perfect?'[22]

More recent times

As we come to our own time, I have selected certain writers who, it seems to me, have made a contribution to our understanding of prayer.

Abbot Columba Marmion

Columba Marmion (1858–1923) was an Irishman who entered the Belgian abbey of Maredsous in 1886, and from 1909 until his death was the Abbot. He was the author of a series of spiritual conferences, the most famous of which was *Christ, The Life of the Soul* in 1918 which ran to over 100,000 copies. He was beatified by Pope John Paul II in 2000.

In *Christ, The Life of the Soul* he treats of the matter of mental prayer 'for attaining union with God here below and being made like to Christ Jesus'.[23] He defines prayer as 'The intercourse of the child of God with his heavenly Father ... is like the expression of our intimate life as children of God, like the outcome of our Divine sonship in Christ, the spontan-eous blossoming of the gifts of the Holy Ghost.'[24]

The means by which this takes place is the action of the Holy Spirit, the Spirit of adoption, 'whom God sends into the hearts of those whom he predestines to be His children in Christ Jesus'.[25]

But this is a conversation not a monologue – one both speaks and listens, 'The soul gives itself up to God, and God communicates Himself to the soul.'[26] But the actual conversation depends on the measure of grace given by Christ and the state of the individual soul. God grants his grace, tailored to each individual. It follows that no particular method of prayer should be prescribed for everyone but each should 'consider their aptitudes, their dispositions, tastes, aspirations and kind of life and take into account the progress they have made in spiritual ways ... Method is one thing, prayer another'.[27] Marmion gives a succinct summary of the gradual ascent of prayer:

> At the beginning, then, of its seeking after God, the soul ought to store up intellectual principles and knowledge of our faith. Why? Because, without that, one will not know what to say and the prayer will degenerate into vague reverie, without depth or fruit, or else will become an exercise full of weariness that the soul will soon abandon. This knowledge has first of all to be stored up; then, afterwards, maintained, renewed and increased. How is this to be done? 'By applying oneself for some time, with the aid of a book, to prolonged reflection on some point of Revelation ... This purely discursive work ought not to be confounded with prayer. It is only the introduction, useful and necessary to enlighten, guide, render pliant or sustain the intelligence, but an introduction all the same. Prayer only begins at the moment when the will, set on fire with love, enters supernaturally into contact with the Divine Good, yielding itself lovingly to God in order to please Him and fulfil His precept and desire. It is in the heart that prayer essentially dwells.'[28]

When we go beyond the initial stages we come to the realm of pure faith, 'passing successively through the sphere of the senses and imagination, of intellectual notions and revealed symbols'.[29] Marmion says this is the beginning of the prayer of quiet where the soul remains recollected in God, feeling united to Him in spite of the darkness.

But, in order to set out on the journey we must be truly detached in mind and heart. We must also be recollected and concentrate on the matter at hand, not half-hearted. Even though we may be troubled by distractions during prayer we do not allow ourselves to be overwhelmed by them. We must also be reverent in the presence of our God who is all holy and we are unworthy servants (see Luke 17:10). But we have an advocate with the Father, Jesus Christ,

> When therefore, we come into God's presence, let us certainly be mistrustful of ourselves, but still more let us arouse our faith in the power that Christ, our Head and Elder Brother, has to bring us near to his Father, who is our Father likewise.[30]

Dom Anselm Rutherford

As a monk of Downside Abbey, Fr Rutherford published his *Acts for Mental Prayer* in 1921. He explains that 'The reasoning employed in meditation is but a means to the production by the soul of acts which shall to some extent effect the union between the soul and God.' He therefore provides a series of short sentences to prompt our prayer, divided into General, Liturgical, the Psalms and Holy Communion. Under General he gives such phrases as: 'Grant me to persevere to the end, faithful and constant in your service'; 'Be always present to me, for I sincerely love you'; 'Fullness of joy, deliver me from all inordinate sadness'; 'May I love you with courage and for your sake endure all difficulties.' The other sections consist of prayers taken from the Liturgy or the Psalms and short aspirations for use after Communion. St John of the Cross comments,

> It should be known that the practice of beginners is to meditate and make acts and discursive reflection with the

imagination. A person in this state should be given matter for meditation and discursive reflection, and he should by himself make interior acts and profit in spiritual things from the delight and satisfaction of the senses.[31]

St Josemaría Escrivá de Balaguer

As a priest, Monsignor Escrivá (1902–1975) worked as a chaplain and university lecturer in Madrid in those years before the outbreak of the Civil War. In 1928 he founded Opus Dei to promote the sanctification of work in the workplace, without changing one's state of life. He also began to formulate 'acts' for meditation which eventually became *The Way* (Camino).[32] St Josemaría was canonized by Pope John Paul II in 2002.

The Way combines the sense of urgency in Ignatius with the appeal of a missionary preacher urging his listeners to be saints,

> You have the obligation to sanctify yourself. Yes, even you! Who thinks this is the exclusive concern of priests and religious? To everyone, without exception, our Lord said: 'Be ye perfect, as my heavenly Father is perfect.' Jesus is never satisfied 'sharing'. He wants all. Don't say, 'That's the way I am – it's my character.' It's your *lack of character*. Be a man.[33]

At the same time there is that sympathy for personal weakness born out of his contact with students, 'Don't worry too much about what the world calls victories or defeats. How often the "victor" ends up defeated!' And again, 'Don't be disheartened. I have seen you struggle. Today's defeat is training for the final victory.'[34] Escrivá, like Brother Lawrence, urges, 'Put yourself in the presence of God, and as soon as you have said,

"Lord, I don't know how to pray!" you can be sure you've already begun.' When it comes to the subject of prayer, he is also down-to-earth,

> You wrote to me: 'To pray is to talk with God. But about what?' About him, and yourself: joys, sorrows, successes and failures, great ambitions, daily worries – even your weaknesses! And acts of thanksgiving and petitions – and love and reparation. In short, to get to know him and to get to know yourself ... The prayer of a Christian is never a monologue.[35]

The success of this little book – it has sold over four million copies – makes it a worthy successor to the other classics of the spiritual life.

Fr Yves Raguin

Fr Raguin (1912–1998) studied at the Harvard School of Oriental Languages. He taught in Shanghai and Vietnam and became Jesuit Superior in Saigon in 1960. His book *How to Pray Today* was published in 1973. From his contact with Oriental religion and his scientific background, he poses new questions on prayer. He argues,

> Christian prayer teaches us to discover the world Christ has revealed to us and to live in it as naturally as we live in the world of men. What we have to learn if we want to pray is that we must move continually from the world in which we live into that world of faith which Christ came to reveal to us.[36]

At the same time we must not be snobs in our prayer, having contempt for the piety of the masses, 'In the liturgy rich and poor meet on the same level.' And it is the poor and frequently superstitious 'who knows only the

Our Father and the *Hail Mary* [but] prays as best he can at Mass and keeps quiet when he cannot understand, and yet, without knowing how, he slowly discovers the vast treasures within the mystery of God. He has entered God's house through the door that is always open to the humble'.[37]

But for those who are troubled by the seeming absence of God in the world surrounding them and the doubts that arise within their own hearts, Raguin says we should make of that a prayer, 'Why not try to develop the readiness to pray by using what we can understand of the enigma of ourselves together with a simple acknowledgement of our link with God?'[38] He insists that we must keep a period of quiet every day to keep in touch with God but this must be allowed to flow over into our work, 'Actions performed through God, in a state of union with Him, that is, in a state of perfect prayer, are at one and the same time both complete rest and full activity ... A saint engrossed in the most exuberant activity always has the core of his being still and tranquil in God.'[39] He adds, 'What has to be avoided, is cutting off our prayer from our life, for that would be to regard our existence as a sea of sorrow to be crossed as best we can ... The whole of [life] should be the very fabric, basis and content of our prayer.'[40]

The *Catechism of the Catholic Church*

First published in 1994 at the request of the synod of bishops, the Catechism devotes its fourth section to prayer (like the previous *Roman Catechism* of the Council of Trent).

The *Roman Catechism* divided prayer into three

degrees: the prayer of faith 'soaring towards heaven', the prayer of penitential sorrow and the prayer of desire of those who do not possess faith.[41] In contrast the *Catechism of the Catholic Church* describes prayer as God's gift, Covenant and Communion and traces the theme through the Scriptures and the Liturgy. It devotes paragraphs to the forms of prayer: Adoration, Petition, Intercession, Thanksgiving and Praise.[42] It then considers the expressions of prayer: Vocal, Meditation and Contemplative Prayer. On Meditation it says, 'We are usually helped by books.' It interprets this widely: 'The Sacred Scriptures, holy icons, liturgical texts of the season, writings of the Fathers, works of spirituality, the great book of creation, and that of history – the page on which the "today" of God is written.'[43] It points out,

> To the extent that we are humble and faithful, we discover in meditation the movements that stir the heart and we are able to discern them ... Meditation engages thought, imagination, emotion and desire. This mobilization of faculties is necessary in order to deepen our convictions of faith, prompt the conversion of our heart and strengthen our will to follow Christ.[44]

In a lyrical passage which many have not read, the Catechism says that Contemplative Prayer 'is like entering into the Eucharistic liturgy: we "gather up" the heart, recollect our whole being under the prompting of the Holy Spirit, abide in the dwelling place of the Lord which we are, awaken our faith in order to enter into the presence of him who awaits us ... It is the simplest expression of the mystery of prayer. It is a *gift*, a grace; it can be accepted only in humility and poverty'.[45]

Notes

1. *Introduction to the Devout Life*, Part 2, chapter 1.
2. Ibid., chapter 10.
3. Ibid., chapter 9.
4. Ibid., chapter 12.
5. *Spiritual Exercises*, p. 21.
6. There is an eight-day version. The term *week* is used loosely; this does not mean that each week must cover a seven-day period.
7. *Fourth Day*, p. 75.
8. n. 12.
9. Cross, p. 898.
10. *Directory*, 37, n. 7.
11. Lercaro, p. 88.
12. Meschler, vol. 1, p. 231.
13. *Spiritual Principles*.
14. Lawrence, *3rd Conversation*, pp. 27-8.
15. Thérèse of Lisieux (1873-1897) *Autobiography*, p. 289.
16. Pourrat, vol. 4, p. 165n.
17. Grou, *How to Pray*, pp. 75-7.
18. Ibid., p. 96.
19. Ibid., p. 109.
20. Ibid., p. 121.
21. Ibid., p. 134.
22. Ibid., p. 159.
23. Marmion, chapter 10, p. 301.
24. Ibid., pp. 302-5.
25. Ibid., p. 305.
26. Ibid., p. 306.
27. Ibid., p. 309.
28. Ibid., pp. 310-11.
29. Ibid., p. 315.
30. Ibid., p. 320.
31. *Living Flame of Love*, Stanza 3 n. 32.
32. First published in Spain in 1934; additional points for meditation were published posthumously as *The Furrow* and *The Forge*.
33. nn 291, 155.
34. nn 415, 263.
35. nn 90, 91, 1154.
36. *How to Pray*, pp. 21, 29.
37. Ibid., p. 33.
38. Ibid., p. 35.

39. Ibid., p. 44.
40. Ibid., p. 48.
41. *Roman Catechism*, chapter 3, nn 4, 5.
42. Ibid., nn. 2559–2643.
43. Ibid., n. 2705.
44. Ibid., nn. 2706, 2708.
45. Ibid., nn. 2711, 2713.

Chapter 6

Pray as You Can and Not as You Can't

> There are many paths on this spiritual road
> Teresa of Avila, *Book of the Foundations*

Prayer for many is daunting. It is the idea of stepping into the unknown and surrendering ourselves to God who may ask impossible things of us. Then we wonder what special techniques we will need to engage in this new practice. There are no special requirements except the resolution to set out on the journey.

From what has already been said, prayer is very individual. God is inviting *you* in particular with all your virtues and weaknesses, your habits and your eccentricities. He wants *your* prayer, whether you are in church or at home or at work, but it is *you* he is talking with. The important thing is that you pray as you can and not as you can't.

Meditation

Most people think meditation is something difficult or exotic; they link it with bio-feedback and self-hypnosis and regard it as a means of escaping modern stress: emptying the mind of negative impressions and tapping into one's whole spiritual wellbeing. Even in the fifties Catholic writers used to talk in terms of *mental prayer*, of which meditation was a part. They then divided mental prayer into a purely intellectual exercise or one in which the will and affections predominate.[1] This already puts people off! Goodier points out,

> There are those, St Teresa explicitly says she is not one of them, who would claim that prayer is a matter of the will alone, that the intellect, at best, is only a preliminary, does but prepare the way for prayer, and should be separated from it. Apart from the fact that in man intellect and will are materially inseparable, there seem objections to this limitation of the meaning of prayer, defined by the masters as 'the raising of the mind to God', and not the will alone.[2]

The *Catechism of the Catholic Church* places the emphasis on the mind when using the term 'meditation': 'It is above all a quest. The mind seeks to understand the why and how of the Christian life, in order to adhere and respond to what the Lord is asking.'[3] The will is obviously there but the initial stages of prayer exercise the mind directly, 'involving reasoning and reflection'.[4] If we use an agricultural analogy, it is digging the soil before putting in the plants.

There is a temptation to forego the spadework rather in the same way that we tend to disregard the instructions when we get a new appliance and then spend hours looking for them when things go wrong. We ought to begin by meditating and try and make a good job of it. St Teresa is quite explicit, 'It is most essential for all Christians to begin this practice. No one, however desperate his case may be, ought to neglect it, if God invites him to make use of it.'[5] Notice that Teresa says that we should *begin* with meditation – not that we should necessarily be so stuck with it that we cannot progress if God prompts us to go further.

The Ignatian method of meditation has become justifiably renowned. It provides material for the mind to exercise itself and at the same time point it in a certain direction. The temptation in prayer, as in many disciplines, is to try and run before we can walk. Meditation is a discipline. Disciplines impose a certain structure which are for our own good. If we are wise we will keep to the guidelines which meditation imposes and in this way not squander our mind on needless distractions and vague musings and dead ends. St Teresa points out, 'If anyone tries to pass beyond this stage and lift up his spirit so as to experience consolations which are not being given to him, I think he is losing both in the one respect and in the other.'[6]

Previous centuries saw numerous books of meditations which have faded like the leaves on the trees.[7] They imposed rather too much on the individual. However we may have gone to the other extreme. *Acts* or *Points* for meditation have a certain value – hence the popularity of *The Way*. But we can take up the words of Scripture, especially the Psalms or the Gospels – maybe the texts used in the daily liturgy – and find them useful launch pads for what should be our *conversation*.

Meditation is not a project on which we will be marked. It is a *means* for us to engage in 'frequent solitary conversation with Him Who we know loves us';[8] 'If we can, we should occupy ourselves in looking upon him who is looking at us; keep him company: talk to him, pray to him.'[9] What Ignatius terms the *colloquy* and St Francis de Sales, the *bouquet* is an expression of that communion. But do not expect too much of a *means*. When the correct height has been reached, the launch vehicle will be jettisoned. There will almost certainly be a time, if we persevere in this type of prayer for meditation not only to lose its natural attraction but also to 'wear out'. When this happens, we must not hang on to meditation like grim death. In time the role played by our reasoning faculty will give way to a meditation in which love predomin-ates and the conversation aspect assumes greater importance.* There is no sudden transition but Aumann counsels that we mustn't leave meditation 'too quickly or too late', and allow ourselves to be open to 'movements of love'.[10]

Ignatius considered, 'One hour [of daily prayer] was sufficient for those engaged in study, provided they have mortification and self-denial.'[11] Cardinal Bernadin agreed, 'What I have found as time has gone on is that the effect of that first hour doesn't end when the hour is up. That hour certainly unites me with the Lord in the early part of the day, but it keeps me connected to him throughout the rest of the day as well.'[12]

Lectio Divina

St Francis de Sales tells Philothea, 'Always keep by you some good book of devotion ... and read a little every day.'[13] The *Lectio Divina* was originally for monks, 'the meditative study of the spiritual Fathers and particularly of the Scriptures'.[14]

We are not reading for the sake of reading, but using the practice to help us to pray. Lercaro defines *Lectio Divina* 'as reading performed slowly and with reflection, interrupted from time to time in order to give scope to good reflection, devout affections or to some vocal prayers'.[15] We need therefore to read a portion of some spiritual book every day – either one of the 'classics' – St Francis de Sales mentions St Bonaventure, Teresa of

---

* See Appendix 1 for some methods of meditation.

Avila and Augustine's *Confessions* – or a more recent work. We should not try to get to the end of each chapter but read until we find a natural pause to allow us to use that thought in prayer. The *Imitation* says 'Read so as to soften the heart, not so as to divert the mind.'[16] *Lectio Divina* 'is not abstract, cold speculation, nor mere human curiosity, nor shallow study; but solid, profound, and persevering investigation of Truth itself . . . It is a study pursued in prayer and in love. The name *lectio* is only the first moment of an ascending series'.[17] In fact there should be no disruption between meditation, reading and contemplation because we should not be compartmentalizing our prayer but allowing it to be led by the Spirit to the heights.

The Jesus Prayer

For Eastern Christianity one particular prayer stands out, *The Jesus Prayer*: 'Lord Jesus Christ, Son of God, have mercy on me [a sinner].' *The Manual of Eastern Orthodox Prayers* adds, 'It is said by devout Christians at regular intervals during the day and the night and is used by them as the basis of their meditation.' It is first found in the sixth-century *Life* of Abba Philemon. Many saints see it strengthening us,

> For when we invoke Jesus, God and Son of God, constantly and tirelessly, he does not allow [the demons] to project in the mind's mirror even the first hint of their infiltration – that is to say, their provocation – or any form, nor does he allow them to have any converse with the heart.[18]

The monks see *The Jesus Prayer* as both protection and warmth for the heart so that it can be on fire with the love of God,

> Moreover, when your intellect is firmly established in your heart, it must not remain there silent and idle, it should constantly repeat and meditate upon the prayer, 'Lord Jesus Christ, Son of God, have mercy on me,' and should never stop doing this. For this prayer protects the intellect from distraction, renders it impregnable to diabolic attacks, and every day increases its love and desire for God.[19]

For some there is a 'physical method' attached to the prayer – the head bowed, eyes fixed on the place of the heart and careful control of breathing – but this appears in the fourteenth century.[20] It strongly recalls postures (*asanas*) which can be found in hatha yoga: in which the yogi sits on a tiger skin, symbolizing energy, overlaid with a deerskin symbolizing calm – with legs crossed in such a way that each foot rests soloe upon its opposing thigh, the spine erect and hands placed palm up in the lap, with appropriate rhythmic breathing.[21] It has always been understood that such exercises 'aim at nothing short of emptying the mind. This void is not actually wanted for its own sake, but it is firmly believed – following the experience of the masters –that, once the mind is emptied and the mental processes stopped, the deep power or light which normally lies hidden and inactive within every man rises up and shines forth by itself'.[22] But such physical activities can become an end in themselves unless we fill the void with the presence of God and have that humility which does not regard ourselves as in any way better than the next person.[23] But in principle, there is no harm in achieving calmness and concentration as an aid to meditation. However, Evagrius counsels, 'Do not pray only with outward forms and gestures, but with reverence and awe try to make your intellect conscious of spiritual prayer.'[24]

Unceasing prayer

The Eastern Fathers are equally committed to the idea of unceasing prayer. They argue that,

> When the Spirit takes its dwelling-place in a man he does not cease to pray because the Spirit will constantly pray in him. Then, neither when he sleeps, nor when he is awake, will prayer be cut off from his soul; but when he eats and when he drinks, when he lies down or when he does any work, even when he is immersed in sleep, the perfumes of prayer will breathe in his heart spontaneously.[25]

Theodorus adds, 'Whatever a man loves, he desires at all costs to be near to continuously and uninterruptedly, and he turns himself away from everything that hinder him from being in contact and dwelling with the object of his love.'[26]

Instead of trying to fathom how one can be meditating continuously while doing the washing-up, we should concentrate on excluding from our thoughts anything which repudiates the presence of God within us. Some, but not all Eastern Fathers, would link such a state of prayer with *dispassion* or freedom from conceptual thoughts altogether. This would seem to prevent those starting out on the journey of prayer from a continual awareness of God's presence which is at the heart of unceasing prayer. It would seem quite possible for people to take to heart the words of St Francis de Sales:

> God is not only present in the place where you are, but also in a very special way, in the depths of your soul, which he enlightens and sanctifies by his presence, since he is, as it were, the heart of your heart, the soul of your soul. Just as the soul is present in every part of the body and yet resides in a special way in the heart, so God, though present every-

where, is present in a special way in the soul ... by considering this truth you will awaken in your heart a great reverence for God, who is so intimately present there.[27]

St Augustine says

[Continuous prayer] is the desire of the heart. And so, if, whatever else you may do, you long for the Sabbath [see Heb. 4:9], then your prayer will have no end. If you wish to pray without end, then keep the desire of your heart alive. The continuation of your longing is the continuation of your prayer. If you no longer love, then your prayer, too, will end.[28]

Raguin proposes a method which has much to recommend it. He says that it is not practicable, unless we are in a religious community on the hour every hour, nor is it advisable. He argues instead that we should perfect the idea to turn to God with 'a quick interior act of praise, of adoration or of gratitude to make very real our immersion in unceasing prayer'. He then confusingly goes on to say that this kind of prayer remains difficult to achieve 'for it counts on the integration of our world and the world of faith and that is something which cannot be achieved without a long experience of the depths of the spiritual life'.[29] He does not seem to be familiar with the aspirations or short prayers piercing heaven, familiar to readers of the *Cloud of Unknowing*. These are by no means the province of the advanced spiritual souls. *The Way* says, 'Make it a habit to raise your heart to God, in acts of thanksgiving, many times a day. Because he gives us this and that ... Because someone has despised you ... Because you don't have what you need, or because you do have it.'[30]

Prayer of the present moment

St Paul reminds us, 'At the acceptable time I have listened to you, and helped you on the day of salvation. Behold, now is the acceptable time, now is the day of salvation' (2 Cor 6:2). There is such a thing as the prayer of the present moment which is linked to the idea of unceasing prayer and to what the Eastern Fathers call *attentiveness*. Fr Grou says that God 'asks of us, in the first place, a constant attention to what is passing in our own hearts, and to His voice which will speak to us there'.[31] St Josemaría makes the point,

> There are no bad or inopportune days. All days are good, for serving God. Days become bad only when men spoil them with their lack of faith, their laziness and their indolence, which turns them away from working with God and for God. 'At all times I will bless the Lord' (Ps 34:2). Time is a treasure that melts away. It escapes from us, slipping through our fingers like water through the mountain rocks. Tomorrow will soon be another yesterday. Our lives are so short. Yesterday has gone and today is passing by. But what a great deal can be done for the love of God in this short space of time![32]

The lament of the psalmist was, 'O that *today* you would listen to his voice ...' (Ps 95:7). We need to realize that God lives in an eternal *now* – yesterday, today and forever. We must not live either in the past or in the future but in the present moment in God's presence. We need to pray to him as we are in that very moment of our existence, knowing that we are precious to him and he wants us to appreciate the importance of each moment.

We must place ourselves not only in the hands of God when we pray but also in the hand of Our Lady and the angels who constantly behold the face of God. The time we spend in prayer is never lost, if we come with a humble and pure heart, as Augustine says, 'this tiny part of all your created desires to please you'.[33]

Vocal prayers

Raguin relates that official Confucianism utterly despised popular piety.[34] Unfortunately among some in the West, a similar opinion prevails. The Pharisees displayed the same sentiments when they told the officers sent to arrest Jesus, 'This rabble know nothing about the law, they are damned' (John 7:49).

Both *Catechisms* (The Tridentine and the most recent) discuss vocal prayer. The *Roman Catechism* drawing on St Thomas Aquinas, says that 'it has its own proper utility *and necessity*: it quickens the attention of the mind, and inflames the devotion of the suppliant'.[35] The *Catechism of the Catholic Church* is even more emphatic,

> Vocal prayer is an essential element of the Christian life ... The need to involve the senses in interior prayer corresponds to a requirement of our human nature. We are body and spirit, and we experience the need to translate our feelings externally. We must pray with our whole being to give all power possible to our supplication.[36]

The same provisos which apply to meditation apply with even stronger force to vocal prayer. Jesus himself demanded, 'Do not babble as the pagans do, for they think that by using many words they will make themselves heard. Do not be like them; your Father knows what you need before you ask him' (Matt 6:7-9). But those words must not be used as a shibboleth to attack the whole concept of vocal prayer. If we vocalize our prayer with devotion, we are meditating. The *Catechism of the Catholic Church* points out, 'Christian prayer tries above all to meditate on the mysteries of Christ, as in lectio divina or the rosary. This form of prayerful reflection is of great value.' But it adds, 'Christian prayer should go further: to the knowledge of the love of the Lord Jesus, to union with him.'[37] Our prayer must never stand still. At each stage we must cooperate with the grace of God and desire to climb further up the mountain.

Notes

1. Lercaro, p. 1.
2. Goodier, p. 147.
3. n. 2705.
4. Lercaro, p. 1.
5. *Way of Perfection*, chapter 16.
6. *Life*, chapter 12.
7. de Cisneros produced his *Ejercitatorio de la vida espiritual* in 1492.
8. *Life*, chapter 8.
9. *Life*, chapter 13.
10. Aumann, p. 324.
11. *Scripta de San Ignacio*, vol. 1, p. 278.
12. Bernadin, p. 97.
13. Francis de Sales, Part 2, chapter 17.
14. Vaggagini, p. 758.
15. Lercaro, p. 195.
16. *Imitation*, Book 1, chapter 20.
17. Lercaro, p. 18.
18. St Hesychios, *On Watchfulness & Holiness*, n. 174.
19. Nikiphorus the Monk, 'On Watchfulness and The Guarding of the Heart' in Philokalia, *The Eastern Christian Spiritual Texts*, vol. 4, p. 65.
20. Cross, p. 738.
21. Smith, H., p. 45.
22. Abhishiktananda, pp. 39–40.
23. Raguin, p. 52.
24. *On Prayer*, n. 28.

25. St Isaac the Syrian (d. 700) quoted in Ware, *The Orthodox Church*, p. 313.
26. St Theodore the Great Ascetic (? 9th century), *A Century of Spiritual Texts*, n. 69.
27. Francis de Sales, Part 2, chapter 2.
28. Explanation of Ps. 38.
29. Raguin, p. 41.
30. *The Way*, n. 268; see also n. 92: 'Throw on the branches and twigs of small vocal prayers, of aspirations, to keep the bonfire burning.'
31. Grou, p. 82.
32. *Friends of God*, p. 43.
33. *Confessions*, Book 1, 1.
34. Raguin, p. 32.
35. Part 4, chapter 8, n.2. Cf. *Summa Theologica*, 2-2 q 83 a. 12.
36. n. 2701. 2.
37. n. 2708.

Chapter 7

Climbing the Mountain

> Who shall climb the mountain of the Lord? Who shall stand in his holy place?
>
> Psalm 24:3

When Sheikh Mujibur-ur-Rahman (1922–1975) became President of Bangladesh in 1971 he was well aware of the path ahead and said, 'I hope for the best, but I prepare for the worst.' Unfortunately, the worst happened ...* Just as we must make our preparations before entering into prayer, so also we must be aware of what lies ahead.

Aridity in prayer

The problem of distractions was already mentioned in Chapter 2. They are like the inconvenience of the mosquito when we are trying to get to sleep, or the neighbour's television heard through the wall. A more unexpected experience is *aridity* or dryness and the inability to pray.

St Teresa, returning to her analogy of watering the garden, says that dryness in prayer can go with 'dislike, distaste and so little desire to go and draw water that he would give it up entirely'.[1] To the extent that he 'seems

---

* He was assassinated in 1975.

to forget God himself'.[2] But she quickly counters by saying,

> What, then, as I say, will the gardener do here? He will be glad and take heart and consider it the greatest of favours to work in the garden of so great an Emperor; and, as he knows that he is pleasing Him by so working (and his purpose must be to please, not himself, but Him), let him render Him great praise for having placed such confidence in him, when He has seen that, without receiving any recompense, he is taking such great care of that which He had entrusted to him, let him help Him to bear the Cross and consider how He lived with it all His life long; let him not wish to have his kingdom on earth or ever cease from prayer; and so let him resolve, even if this aridity should persist his whole life long, never to let Christ fall beneath the Cross.[3]

The most common remark to hear from people who persevere in prayer is that they are getting nothing out of it, or they are getting nowhere. This is aridity and we should treat it as we treat distractions – only as more lasting and more annoying! We need to take St Teresa's advice and put our trust in God who allows us to spend this time with him as he permitted Peter, James and John to share his prayer in the Garden of Gethsemani even though they could not keep awake.

The first 'night'

It will also help if we realize that such dryness is part of the process of climbing the mountain of prayer. Unlike a real mountain, it is an ascent into increasing darkness and blindness. Walter Hilton says, 'Open your heart then to the movement of grace and accustom yourself to dwell in this darkness, strive to become familiar with it.'[4] To live in this darkness may feel that we are far from God, but we will find that our love for God is deeper and stronger in the process as The *Cloud of Unknowing* points out,

> Reconcile yourself to wait in this darkness as long as is necessary, but still go on longing after him whom you love. For if you are to feel him or to see him in this life it must always be in this cloud, in this darkness.[5]

St John of the Cross talks in terms of three stages of darkness, or *Nights* through which we must pass on our journey. He says that 'The first part, which is that of the sense, is comparable to the beginning of night, the point at which things begin to fade from sight.'[6] If St John were alive today he might make use of rocket technology to talk in terms of the need for the first stage to fall away so that the command module could continue on into space. This 'detachment' is necessary so that we can advance on the journey. The Eastern Fathers talk in terms of a circumcision of the heart which involves 'the utter stripping away from the senses and the intellect of their natural activities concerning sensible and intelligible things'. Moreover, Maximos adds, 'This stripping away is accomplished by the Spirit's immediate presence.'[7] We have to accept that we live most of our lives at the level of our senses and allow them often far too much rein. If we are to enter into the realm of the spirit then we have to suffer a diminution of the hold which the senses have so that we can respond to the Spirit. We share this with Islam for before prayer a ritual ablution is performed to ensure that each is in a state of spiritual as well as physical purity and the mind is cleansed and healed from worldly thoughts and concerns concentrated on God.

We need also to recognize that there remains that craving for sensual satisfaction that must be damped down or it will arrest the progress of our prayer altogether, and this is gradually accomplished by the experience of aridity.

At the same time we have to accustom our minds to that realization that we cannot truly *know* God in the human sense because he is so above our understanding: 'Though we speak much we cannot reach the end, and the sum of our words is: "he is the all" (Sir 43:27).' Beyond words and beyond our mind to comprehend. St Anselm approaches the mystery saying,

> My soul strives to see more, and it sees nothing beyond what it has seen except darkness, for there is no darkness in you, but it sees that it cannot see more *because of its own darkness*. Truly Lord this is the inaccessible light in which you dwell.[8]

St John of the Cross talks in terms of incomprehension and blindness, 'In order to reach God it is necessary to go by way of incomprehension and being blind and placed in darkness the eyes are opened to reach towards the divine light.'[9]

There is a parallel in the approach of Zen Buddhism. Huston rightly says that in the West, 'We rely on reason so fully that we must remind ourselves that in Zen we are dealing with a perspective that is convinced that reason is limited and must be supplemented by another mode of reasoning.'[10] This is accomplished by the use of contradictory riddles or *koans* – for instance: 'What was the appearance of your face before your ancestors were born?' Our impulse is to dismiss these puzzles as absurd but the whole point is to bring the mind to go beyond logic. In Zen of course the journey ends within whereas in Christianity we go within in order to journey into the boundless majesty of God: we come to know the invisible in us so that we can come to know the invisible which is God.[11]

Consolations

As counterpoint to aridity, there are consolations. In fact at one moment we can be experiencing complete dryness of spirit and at another great warmth and sweetness. Some spiritual writers are very hard on consolations and tend to regard them in the same breath as insidious temptations. The *Cloud of Unknowing* regards them as hors d'oevres rather than the main course,

> As a foretaste of that heavenly reward he will on occasion inflame the actual body of his devout servant – and not once or twice but perhaps often, and when he likes – with very wonderful sweetness and consolation ... Such comfort and sweetness should not be held suspect, and, to say no more, I believe that he who enjoys it cannot regard it so.[12]

The fact that they surpass the greatest of any earthly pleasure is meant to encourage us with a longing for heavenly things: 'the sugar plums by which God attracts his little ones; the health-giving waters by which he strengthens them'.[13] St Francis de Sales also points out, 'Such feelings may be experienced by those who are still attached to sin and who consequently have no true love for good, much less any true devotion.'[14] We must not put too great an emphasis on consolations so that we luxuriate in them because we are mistaking the means for the end. St John of the Cross remarks,

> Some wander about in search only of sweetness and delightful communication from God. Such an attitude is not the hallmark of self-denial and nakedness of spirit, but the indication of a 'spiritual sweet tooth' ... He sometimes condescends to the petition of certain individuals, for since they are good and simple, he does not like to let them go unanswered, lest they become sad.[15]

Consolations are incidental markers on the journey; they are not part of the journey itself. We should take them as they come and thank God for them but St John warns us:

> Some souls obtain spiritual sweetness from God because they are incapable of eating the stronger and more solid food of the trials of the Cross of His Son. He would desire them to take the Cross more than any other thing.[16]

Spiritual directors who have to insinuate such thoughts frequently find the response, 'This is a hard saying; who can listen to it?' (John 6:60). It is human to like sugar plums but a diet of continual saccharin will make us self-indulgent to the extent that we forget about the journey of prayer altogether.

We must have as a companion on our journey of prayer true humility, which is willing to reveal weaknesses as well as consolations to our confessor or spiritual director. This will avoid any false sense of self-importance. But a clear sign that we are on the right road, is our continuing love of our neighbour,

> One act done in charity is more precious in God's sight than all the visions and communications possible – *since they imply neither merit nor demerit* – and how many who have not received these experiences are incomparably more advanced than others who have had many.[17]

We are not aiming for a Confucian detachment or the experience of *satori* but an ascent towards him who loves us as he loves all who are created in the image of his Son, and wants us to share in that love,

> Have the same thoughts, sharing the same love, and being one in soul and mind. Do not do anything from selfish ambition, or from a cheap desire to boast, but be humble towards each other, never thinking you are better than others. (Phil 2:2–4)

Spiritual direction

In the matter of consolations especially, such a person as a spiritual director is essential. The old adage is *Nemo iudex sua causa* (Nobody is a judge in his own case). We may think either that we are called by God to some special work or that we are mired in sin and unworthy to embark on prayer at all. A spiritual director will help to clarify the issue.

Unfortunately, the decline in the practice of the Sacrament of Penance and Reconciliation means that the concept of Direction has become somewhat alien. St Teresa of Avila is as forthright as always, 'The beginner needs counsel to help him ascertain what benefits him most. To this end a director is very necessary.'[18]

We would conjecture that the holy abbess would recommend a man of devotion. She looks for holiness in a director but insists upon prudence and learning. By learning she means a grasp of spiritual theology: 'Men of virtue, skilled in theology and ascetics.'[19] The lack of learning means that either people are 'constrained and afflicted' or they are forced into a spiritual dependency on their director which deprives them of any freedom of initiative, 'If her director is a simpleton and gets the idea into his head, he will give [the nun] to understand that it is better for her to obey him than her superior and he will do this without any evil intention, thinking he is right.'[20] It may surprise people that weighing up spirituality and learning, Teresa opts for learning:

> Let us not make the mistake of saying that learned men who do not practise prayer are not suitable directors for those who do. I have consulted many such; and for some years past, feeling a greater need of them, I have sought them out more ... I have said this because some people think that learned men, if they are not spiritual, are unsuitable for those who practise prayer. I have already said that a spiritual director is necessary, but if he has no learning it is a great inconvenience ... I have also experience of timid, half-learned men whose shortcomings have cost me very dear.[21]

She rather hopes that the learned director might even become more spiritual in the course of time,

> It will help us very much to consult learned men, provided they are virtuous; even if they are not spiritual they will do us good and God will show them what they should teach and may even make them spiritual so that they may be of service to us.[22]

Above all else there must be that allowance for the individual to progress along the path to which God has called them. St John of the Cross insists,

> The director's whole concern should not be to accommodate souls to his own method and condition, but he should observe the road along which God is leading them, and if he does not recognize it, he should leave them alone and not bother them. And in harmony with the path and spirit along which God leads them, the spiritual director should strive to

conduct them into greater solitude, tranquility and freedom of spirit.[23]

Although we must make allowances for the grace of God to raise up directors, there is a problem. Priestly training does not put a high premium on spiritual theology. Partly this is due to pressure on the timetable and partly to a rather irrational fear of the possibility of Quietism: Mysticism: Begins in Mist and ends in Schism. It was about precisely such attitudes that St Teresa warned . . . The fear of falling into error must not be made an excuse to neglect what is surely a justifiable demand of an intelligent member of God's holy Church, namely a guide to help on the journey of prayer and holiness.

We talk of direction as if it was the sole task of an individual, but in fact the real director is the Holy Spirit. It has been one of the contributions of the Charismatic Renewal that such an emphasis has been rediscovered. We need to trust in the Spirit we have received, and let him lead us through those who have allowed themselves to be guided by that same Spirit.[24]

Quietism
It takes its name from 'the prayer of quiet' used by many Christian mystics.* It was seen as the successor to the *Alumbrados* (the Illuminati) – suspicion fell at the time on St Ignatius and St Teresa. Quietism and its principle proponent, Miguel de Molinos, were condemned in 1687 because they stood for such a religious passivity 'that the soul annihilates itself in its power of acting' and in some sense it tended to minimize personal responsibility for

---

* St Teresa, *Spiritual Relations*, 5; *Interior Castle*, Fourth Mansion, chapter 2; *Way of Perfection*, chapter 31.

sin.[25] For this reason, Contemplation itself was seen as a dangerous and unhealthy ambition which should be discouraged.

Notes
1. *Life*, chapter 11.
2. Ibid., chapter 28.
3. Ibid., chapter 11.
4. *Scale of Perfection*, 2, 25. The author became an Augustinian Canon at Thurgarton Priory in Nottingham. He died in 1396.
5. p. 54.
6. *Ascent of Mount Carmel*, 1.2, n. 5. *The Cloud* talks of a cloud *of forgetting* (chapter 5).
7. St Maximos, *First Century on Theology*, n. 46.
8. *Proslogion*, chapter 14, n. 16.
9. *Ascent of Mount Carmel*, 2.8, n. 5.
10. Smith, H., p. 134.
11. Lassalle, p. 137.
12. Chapter 48.
13. Francis de Sales, Book 4, chapter 13.
14. Ibid.
15. *Ascent of Mount Carmel*, Book 2, chapter 7.
16. Ibid., chapter 21.
17. Ibid.
18. Ibid., Book 2, chapter 22.
19. Pius XII, *Discourse February 6, 1940*, Veuillot, vol I.2.p. 42.
20. *Life*, chapter 13.
21. *Life*, chapter 13.
22. Ibid.
23. *Interior Castle*, 5, 1; John of the Cross, *Living Flame of Love*, 3, 30.
24. *Living Flame of Love*, 3, 46.
25. Simon Tugwell, p. 125. Cf. St Teresa's mention of 'half-lettered' spiritual guides, *Interior Castle*, chapter 5.

Chapter 8

The Heights of Prayer

> God is also a dark night to us in this life ... for faith is obscure, like night to the understanding.
> John of the Cross, *Ascent of Mount Carmel*

St John of the Cross calls the first part of the journey the night of sense, 'which concerns the sensory part of man's nature'. The second part 'refers to the night of the spiritual part of man's soul'. This, he describes in poetic terms:

> One dark night,
> Filled with love's urgent longings,
> – Ah the sheer grace! –
> I went out unseen,
> My house being now all stilled.[1]

The journey now begins in earnest in visible darkness. Isaiah can say, 'Truly you are a god who *lies hidden*, the God of Israel, the Saviour'(Isa 45:15). We must journey to this secret place 'in darkness and concealment' now that the house of our senses in stilled.

Entering into the 'night'

Just as it is insulting to the Holy Spirit to continue (discursive) meditation when we are asked to go higher, so it is also imprudent if we start climbing the mountain before we are ready. St John of the Cross provides guidelines. He says that as long as we can make discursive meditation and gain profit from it, we should not give it up. But if we find it increasingly difficult to meditate and we cannot fix our attention on such things as composition of place then we should realize that we are called to a higher form of prayer. But the surest sign is a desire for quiet reflection when:

> A person likes to remain alone in loving awareness of God, without particular considerations, in interior peace and quiet and repose, and without the acts and exercises ... of the intellect, memory and will; and that prefers to remain only in the general, loving awareness and knowledge we mentioned, without any particular knowledge or understanding.[2]

It is obvious that we should make such a decision to abandon meditation, in consultation with our spiritual director. The director himself must not either restrain or urge on impulsively but respect the freedom of the soul in each case and merely prompt the person so that the true state of affairs can be determined.

The dark night of the soul

St Teresa continues her analogy of the garden which gets its water from the river or the brook. She points out,

> In this state our Lord desires to help the gardener in such a way that he may almost be said to be the gardener himself, since he does all the work. The prayer is *a sleep of the faculties of the soul*, which are not wholly lost, nor able to understand how they are at work.[3]

It is in this state that the need for spiritual direction becomes more marked for we are entering into uncharted territory where the familiar landmarks can no longer be found. St Teresa tries to explain the root of the problem,

> We should contrive, not to use our reasoning powers, but to be intent upon discovering what the Lord is working in the soul; for, if His Majesty has not begun to grant us absorption, I cannot understand how we can cease thinking in any way which will not bring us more harm than profit ...When His Majesty wishes the working of the understanding to cease, he employs it in another manner, and illumines the soul's knowledge to so much higher a degree than any we can ourselves attain that he leads it into a state of absorption, in which, without knowing how, it is much better instructed than it could ever be as a result of its own efforts.[4]

We discover when we have entered this stage of prayer that His Majesty, Our Lord and God, is beyond anything we can comprehend with our mind: 'The heavens are as high above the earth, as my ways are above your ways, my thoughts above your thoughts' (Isa. 55:9). God who has taken charge allows the Holy Spirit free rein to direct us in our inmost being.

St John of the Cross says that in this stage 'God teaches the soul secretly and instructs it in the perfection of love without its doing anything nor understanding how this happens.'[5] But it is a *dark* night because we are faced with what St John calls 'the inflow of God into the soul'[6] which plunges the mind into darkness because it cannot grasp the experience rationally. The Eastern Fathers are familiar with this state of prayer and talk in terms of

> The intellect, abandoning all conceptual images of the world, concentrates itself and prays without distraction or

> disturbance *as if God were present, as indeed he is* ... At the very onset of prayer the intellect is so ravished by the divine and infinite light that it is aware neither of itself nor of any other created thing, but only of him who through love has activated such radiance in it.[7]

There is also 'darkness' because of an awareness of imperfection in the face of the total majesty of God. This 'darkness' causes great distress and pain because the soul writhes with pain in our birth-pangs (Isa 26:17) so that it can have God alone. But that pain is magnified because the dark light of God shows up all our innate sinfulness and weakness. St John of the Cross gives an example, 'When eyes are sickly, impure, and weak, they suffer pain if a bright line shines on them.'[8] Job asked God, 'Can you not tolerate my sin, nor overlook my fault?' (Job 7:21). Those who enter this stage of prayer know the answer before they say it. They are overwhelmed by their sense of unworthiness to the point of anguish – which is an anticipation of the sufferings of Purgatory – even as they are conscious that it is the love of God which is the cause of it. He who exalted his Mother Mary 'looked on his servant in her lowliness' (Luke 1:48). He desires that same utter humility and poverty of spirit – indeed the spiritual person sees a new dimension to the Beatitudes – but to reach that point will entail the anguish of being detached from our egoism which continually claims its rights so that we can give ourselves to God.

Desolation

Those who enter into this night must be prepared for a complete lack of consolation which made the earlier stages so pleasant. Here, however, there is desolation of soul. Even his spiritual director cannot bring consolation because the individual cannot believe that God is allowing this out of love. There is only darkness – blind faith, helplessness. St John speaking of personal experience, says,

> He resembles one who is imprisoned in a dark dungeon, bound hands and feet, and able neither to move, nor see, nor feel any favour from heaven or earth. He remains in this condition until his spirit is humbled, softened, and purified, until it becomes so delicate, simple, and refined that it can be one with the Spirit of God, according to the degree of union of love that God, in his mercy, desires to grant.[9]

But as with Purgatory itself, there is no timetable, but 'If it is to be truly efficacious, it will last for some years, no matter how intense it may be.'[10] No consolation there either...

There is also a real sense that one is lost and that we are to be denied the blessings of God forever, which is surely part of the pain of Purgatory.

There was much surprise expressed when it was disclosed that Mother Teresa of Calcutta experienced such abandonment* because people considered that saints always lived in a state of supernatural joy. But Bernadette Soubirous (1804–1879), the saint of Lourdes, penned a prayer, 'You, who have felt the utter desolation of your dear Son, assist me in the hour of mine.'[11] St Thérèse of Lisieux (1873–1897) records,

> God permitted my soul to be covered in thick darkness, and allowed the thought of heaven, which had always been so

---

* Mother Teresa wrote in one of her letters, 'You arrive at enough certainty to be able to make your way, but it is making it in darkness.'

dear to me, to become something which caused me torment and internal conflict ... This trial was not for a matter of a few days, or even weeks, it is something that is destined to go on until God sees fit to have things otherwise.[12]

The fire of God's love

It is highly likely that those whom God calls to holiness are also called to the heights of prayer and the consequent pain which that involves. But as with the pain of Purgatory there is an awareness throughout of the abiding love of God. In a strange way St John says, 'The soul in the midst of these dark conflicts feels vividly and keenly that it is being wounded by a strong divine love ... Yet it understands nothing.'[13] In the dark night the soul is 'fired with love's urgent longings'. God so fills us with his love that we are 'afflicted' by love and wish to be united with the object of our love. So the psalmist cries out, 'My soul is thirsting for God, the God of my life; when can I enter and see the face of God?'(Ps. 42:2).

The night of faith

St John says that this second 'night' is one of faith which almost seems a contradiction in itself for 'Faith is the *substance* of things to be hoped for, the *evidence* of things that appear not' (Heb 11:1). But precisely because faith is *not* sight, and on earth 'we see in a glass darkly' (1 Cor 13:12), faith alone can penetrate to the inner life of God. As St John says,

> The imagination cannot fashion or imagine anything whatever beyond that which it has experienced through the external senses, namely, that which it has seen with the eyes,

heard with the ears, etc. At most, it can only compose likenesses of those things which it has seen or heard or felt ... Just so, all that the imagination can imagine and the intellect can receive and understand in this life is not, nor can it be, a proximate means of union with God.[14]

The individual who is called to this higher state of prayer is summoned to walk in dark and pure faith.

But this darkness is not some cold void or abyss into which we are plunged. We have always with us our Way and our Life, Jesus himself. He has told us, 'No one comes to the Father, except through me' (John 14:6). As Marmion puts it, 'You will never attain to the Divinity save in passing through my humanity.'[15] The pure faith which we are called to possess in this dark night is a faith in the power of his humanity which will allow us to enter with him into the holy of holies, beyond the veil. St Teresa says, 'If we are to please [God], and he is to grant us great favours, then this should be done through his most sacred humanity, in whom his majesty said, he is well pleased.'[16]

St Teresa also provides a glimpse into that faith which 'sees' God,

> When the Lord so wills, it may happen that the soul will be at prayer, and in possession of all its senses, and that then there will suddenly come to it a suspension in which the Lord communicates most secret things to it, which it seems to see within God himself. These are not visions of the most sacred humanity; although I say that the soul 'sees' him, it really sees nothing, for this is not an imaginary, but a notably intellectual, vision, in which is revealed to the soul how all things are seen in God, and how within himself, he contains them all.[17]

St John of the Cross gives us the ordered structure of prayer but St Teresa adds those incidentals which make prayer that much more attractive. It is as if she was listening to St John as her spiritual director, 'my little Seneca' (he was at Avila from 1572–77) and interrupting his theological explanations, with 'Yes, but this happened to me when I was at prayer.' We must not allow prayer to become a theological exercise. Merton points out that 'revelation' and 'knowledge' play a part in Oriental mysticism and that it is far more 'intellectual' and speculative than in the West, but one of its deficiencies is that it is *'too* intellectual'.[18] In Christianity there is such a thing as warmth and joy which comes from our communion with Jesus, the Son made man for us. In prayer we experience his closeness to us and through him we come into the presence of the Father. In this way, Jesus's own final words are fulfilled, 'These have known that you have sent me. I have made your name known to them, so that the love with which you loved me may be in them and so that I may be in them' (John 17:26).

Notes
1. *Ascent of Mount Carmel*, chapter 1, 2.
2. Ibid., chapter 1, 14.
3. *Life*, chapter 16.
4. *Interior Castle*, 4, 3.
5. *Dark Night*, 2, 5.
6. Ibid.
7. Maximos, *Second Century on Love*, n. 6.
8. *Dark Night*, 2, 5.
9. Ibid., 2, 7.
10. Ibid.
11. Trochu, *Bernadette*, p. 322.
12. *St Thérèse By Those who Knew Her*, p. 40.

13. *Dark Night*, 2, 11.
14. Ibid., 1, 9.
15. Marmion, p. 319.
16. *Life*, chapter 22.
17. *Interior Castle*, 6, 10.
18. Merton, p. 50.

Chapter 9

The Living Flame of Love

By your gift we are on fire and borne upwards.
                                Augustine, *Confessions*

St Teresa, talking of the invitation which God gives to call people to the heights of prayer says,

> It is a great gift, much greater than I can say ... I know many souls who attain thus far; and I know, too, that those who go farther as they ought to do, are so few that I am ashamed to confess it ... I should like very much to advise such persons to be careful not to hide their talent, for it would seem that God is pleased to choose them to the advantage of many in these times when He needs his friends to be strong so that they may uphold the weak.[1]

The invitation to go higher is a privilege but also a responsibility. We must not think that prayer is purely personal; it has a profound impact because it allows the Son of God who was born into this world for us and our salvation to continue that work though us.

God gives the invitation and with it the accompanying grace, 'Those whom he called he also justified; and those whom he justified he also glorified' (Rom 8:30). We cannot identify precisely the moment when we pass from the night of the spirit to that final night, 'How this prayer they call union happens and what it is, I cannot explain. Mystical theology explains it, and I am unable to use the proper terms.'[2] St John using the proper terms, says that this final stage is like the close of night and near the light of day. He explains the process again poetically:

> In darkness, and secure,
> By the secret ladder, disguised,
> – Ah, the sheer grace
> In darkness and concealment,
> My house being now all stilled.[3]

The darkness has already been discussed but St John adds *the secret ladder, disguised.* He explains that it must be *secret* because it is infused into the soul through love and how this takes place is part of God's mysterious activity; the soul neither knows nor understands how this comes to pass.[4] It is also a *ladder* because by it 'The soul ascends in order ... to know and possess the goods and treasures of heaven.' But because one can go up and down a ladder, it also produces a feeling of joy and humility from the same experience of the overwhelming love of God.[5] Without humility, contemplation would become self-exaltation. The supreme knowledge of God must be accompanied by a sober knowledge of oneself.

St Bernard of Clairvaux describes the impact of this union in his Commentary on the Song of Songs,

> He moved and mollified and wounded my heart, since it was hard as a rock and desperately ill. And then he began to root up and to destroy, to build and to plant, to water what was parched, to enlighten what was dark, to set free what was chained up, to set on fire what was cold, as well as to set the crooked ways straight and the rough ways plain, so that my soul might bless the Lord, and all that is in me might bless his holy name. Therefore, when the Word and Bridegroom entered into me from time to time, his coming was

never made known by any signs ... it was only from the motion of my heart that I understood he was present. And I recognized the power of his might from the way vices were banished and how carnal desires were repressed. I was in awe at his profound wisdom by the way he uncovered and refuted my hidden sins, and I experienced the goodness of his mercy by even the very slight ways he improved my way of life.[6]

But it is also necessary to have the ladder *disguised*. St John explains that this disguise takes the form of the theological virtues, of faith, hope and charity. Already we experience in the dark night of the spirit the night of faith and we continue with that virtue to strengthen us against our ancient enemy as much as to obtain God's favour.

We also rely on hope because it is the virtue which puts before us the things of eternity so that we no longer set our heart on the things of this world but live only for eternal life. Ignatius of Antioch could write, 'Earthly longings in me have been crucified; in me there is left no part of desire for mundane things, but only a murmur of living water that whis- pers within me, "Come to the Father".'[7] St Bernadette wrote in a firm hand in her private notebook, 'I will do everything for heaven.'[8]

But above all there is the love of God which counteracts any love of self and its need and demands. It centres the will on God alone. Popular fiction tends to describe holy people as drained of all charm and withered in character but those who have climbed this secret ladder become filled with sweetness and grace which makes them attractive and overflows on those they meet. That is the grace of God in action.

As far as the *ladder* is concerned: St John explains that

we progress step by step, or rung by rung. At the beginning there is the continuing awareness of unworthiness due to sin (which does not amount to that dullness of soul which leaves us with a wandering mind[9] but comes from a general revulsion from our sinfulness. We then earnestly desire God, 'I sought him whom my soul loves' (Song 3:1) and want to express it in action, but know that all that one does is far too little. There is no desire for consolations or request for favour but a wish to labour in the service of God who loves us to the point of anguish because we cannot love as much in return.

As we ascend to the top of the ladder we become more eager and more daring and desire to have God and him alone, 'I held him and would not let him go' (Song 3:4). This desire fills our hearts with the warmth of God's love. St Philip Neri (1515–1595) experienced it as a ball of fire while praying in the catacombs of St Sebastian.[10] Such is the power of this love which flies upwards, that at the top of the ladder the soul becomes so united with God that it leaves the body and enters heaven.[11]

Theosis or deification

The doctrine of Theosis or deification is based on the idea of man made in the image of the Holy Trinity. Everyone therefore is called to participate fully in the life of the Triune God (see 2 Pet. 1:4), therefore the Eastern Fathers regard the life of the ordinary Christian as one which leads to Theosis if they give themselves to such a participation. It is a union not with God in his essence but in his divine *energies*, 'God and those who are worthy of God have one and the same energy.'[12] We are called to become illumined with the divine light and his uncreated grace. This light is not only visible to us but we share in it and by it we are deified.[13] Therefore we can say,

> God in his entirety penetrates the saints in their entirety, and the saints in their entirety penetrate God entirely, exchanging the whole of him for themselves, and acquiring him alone as the reward of their ascent toward him, for he embraces them as the soul embraces the body, enabling them to be in him as his own members.[14]

But this is brought about by love, 'Only when it has been made like God insofar, of course, as this is possible – does it bear the divine likeness of love as well.'[15] In the process, we are purified, 'God who yearns for the salvation of all men and hungers for their deification, withers their conceit like the unfruitful fig tree.'[16] In the process we can witness the impact on the whole personality. When Arsenius was praying, his disciples saw him 'just like a fire'[17] and the transfigured face of St Seraphim and that of Abba Pambo, which 'shone lightning'.[18]

The Eastern Fathers also put a premium on the need for continued repentance, never ceasing to use the *Jesus Prayer*. The love of God must naturally be expressed in love for one's neighbour, 'As the three persons of the Godhead "dwell" in each other, so we must "dwell" in our neighbour.'[19] The great Abbot Antony said, 'Our life and our death are with our neighbour. If we do good to our neighbour, we do good to God; if we cause our neighbour to stumble, we sin against Christ.'[20] There is no room for a spiritual journey which avoids that service of others to which our Servant calls us (Luke 22:27) or for an individualism that dispenses with the Commandments, the Scriptures, the Liturgy and the Sacraments of the Church. We are all united in one body which we desire to be transfigured according to the likeness of Christ our head.

The living flame of love

The Discalced Carmelite, Fr Thomas of Jesus, says that once we have entered into this stage of prayer, we may be 'admitted to the kiss of the heavenly Spouse in contemplation'.[21] Mystical writers have made much use of the words of the Song of Songs, 'O that you would kiss me with the kisses of your mouth!' They express that state which has been called in mysticism 'the spiritual betrothal'. How do we know that we have reached this stage? We must have great purity of heart and renunciation of even the slightest sin. We must also be in a state of great self-control through practice of the virtues and we must be in a continual dialogue with God, talking with him and referring everything to him, even in the midst of distractions.[22]

If all these conditions are met then we reach that union with God in which the soul surrenders itself completely and is transformed: 'The bar of iron that is plunged into the fire takes on its fiery qualities; and the soul that plunges itself into God, that most fiery of furnaces, through prayer, is all light and heat, enkindled with intense love.'[23] This brings with it great sweetness which 'greatly surpasses all others, as a river surpasses a drop of water'.[24] If we arrive at this state, says St Teresa, 'Love and faith work together, and the soul has no desire to profit by what the understanding teaches her. For this union which takes place ... has taught her other things which are beyond the grasp of the understanding.'[25] This is a state of such intimacy with God that the person is completely purified of all sensual demands and appetites and has now completely mortified the will, 'having gone out in search at night'. This search is finally ended 'on that glad night' and He who is loved grants us that strength and peace and quietness in Him, 'my house being now all stilled'.[26] Peter had a partial insight into such joy when on the Mount of Transfiguration he could say, 'Lord, it is good that we are here' (Matt 17:2). But Mark adds, 'He hardly knew what to say, they were so terrified' (Mark 9:6). This final stage of prayer makes us even more aware of the awe-inspiring power which is joined at the same time to the love of God, made present in his Son. St Teresa makes her characteristic comment, 'The good Jesus is too good a company for us to forsake him...'[27]

But St Teresa adds, 'The more is revealed to her of how much this great God and Lord deserves to be loved, the more does her love for him grow.'[28] She explains that this causes the fire of love to fill our whole being,

> The soul, then, has these yearnings and tears and sighs, together with the strong impulses which have already been described. They all seem to arise from our love, and are accompanied by great emotion, but they are as nothing by comparison with this other, for they are like a smouldering fire, the heat of which is quite bearable, though it causes pain. While the soul is in this condition and interiorly burning, it often happens that a mere fleeing thought of some kind ... or some remark which the soul hears ... deals it, as it were, a blow, or, as one might say, wounds it with an arrow of fire.[29]

We can be grateful to St Teresa for such a clinical analysis of her experience, although she adds, 'All that I say falls short of the truth, which is indescribable.' But she

The Living Flame of Love 101

has given us an insight into the unspeakable joy which transfixes the soul when it has become united with God in the heights of prayer. Those who talk of being deliriously in love have only an inkling of the experience of mystical union. St Paul, who himself was privileged to be taken up to the seventh heaven could write, 'What eye has not seen, and ear has not heard, and what has not entered the human heart, what God has prepared for those who love him' (1 Cor 2:9).

When God comes to dwell in the soul (as in a second heaven, says St Teresa[30]), the night is exchanged for light. St John talks of the dawn breaking. In this light, God allows the individual to see and understand something of what is happening, whereas before there was almost total obscurity. In Teresa's case,

> The Most Holy Trinity reveals itself, in all three Persons ... It sees these three Persons, individually, and yet, by a wonderful kind of knowledge which is given to it, the soul realizes that most certainly and truly all these three Persons are one Substance and one Power and one Knowledge and one God alone; so that what we hold by faith the soul may be said to grasp by sight ... Here all three Persons communicate themselves to the soul and speak to the soul and explain to it those words which the Gospel attributes to the Lord – namely, that he and the Father and the Holy Spirit will come to dwell with the soul which loves him and keeps his commandments.[31]

This was Teresa's personal experience for what is ultimately beyond explanation. God reveals himself in some sense, 'as he is'. As with Moses, who asked to see his face, he revealed as much as Moses could bear (Exo. 33:17). This recognition stays with the one who is united with God together with a desire never to be offend him in the least way. As with an earthly marriage, it deepens for 'The contemplation of God's face is a never ending journey toward him.'[32]

'He who is joined to God becomes one spirit with him'

In the mystical marriage, there is no awareness of any separation. The Soul remains 'all the time in the centre with its God ... as if a tiny streamlet enters the sea, from which it will find no way of separating itself'.[33] In this final state of prayer the soul becomes aware that it owes its whole life to God and God at the centre of the soul is continually conferring that life. Because of this there is a forgetfulness of self so as to live only for God which is willing to undergo any suffering and rejection for love of him, and take care of never offending him. But all the time it is aware of how little it is able to do for God.

Above all there, must be humility, 'And if you have not true humility, the Lord will not wish it to reach any great height: in fact, it is for your own good that it should not; if it did, it would fall to the ground.'[34] To help in this we should fix our attention on the Cross of Christ. He humbled himself even to accepting death on the Cross.

Notes
1. *Life*, chapter 15.
2. Ibid., chapter 18.
3. *Dark Night*, 2, 15.
4. Ibid., 2, 17.
5. Ibid., 2, 18.
6. *Sermon 74*.
7. Ignatius of Antioch, *Letter to the Romans*, chapter 6.

The Living Flame of Love 103

8. Trochu, *Bernadette*, p. 372.
9. *Dark Night*, 2, 2.
10. Ponnelle & Bordet, pp. 96-7, 129.
11. *Dark Night*, 2, 19, 20.
12. Ambigua, PG 91, 1076c.
13. Gregory Palamas (1296-1359), *Conversation of an Orthodox with a Barlamite*, n. 11.
14. *The Declaration of the Holy Mountain in Defence of Those who Devoutly Practise a Life of Stillness*, n. 2.
15. St Diadochus of Photiki (5th century), *On Spiritual Knowledge & Discrimination*, n. 89.
16. Maximos, *First Century on Various Texts*, n. 7.
17. Sayings of the Fathers: Pambo, n. 12.
18. Ibid., Arsenius, n. 27.
19. Ware, p. 241.
20. Ward, p. 177.
21. Lercaro, p. 258.
22. Ibid., p. 259.
23. Ibid., p. 260. Cf. also the Sufi poet, Rumi, 'Love, too is a furnace/ And ego its fuel'(*Love's Furnace*, line 1377).
24. Thomas of Jesus, pp. 73-4.
25. *Conceptions of the Love of God*, chapter 3.
26. *Dark Night*, 2, 23.
27. *Interior Castle*, 6, 7.
28. Ibid., 6, vii.
29. Ibid.
30. Ibid., 7, 1.
31. Ibid.
32. Gregory of Nyssa (330-395), *Commentary on the Song of Songs*, n. 12.
33. *Interior Castle*, 7, 2.
34. Ibid., 7, 4.

Chapter 10

Certain Mystical Experiences

> We cannot lead this perfect kind of life of ourselves unless the Father draws us.
>
> Francis de Sales, *Treatise of the Love of God*

St Philip Neri, who was no stranger to the heights of contemplation, was heard to say on one occasion, 'He who wishes for ecstasies is deceiving himself greatly, for he does not know what an ecstasy is.'[1]

Ecstasy

Ecstasy – from the Greek, meaning to put a person out of his place – can be applied in the mystical sense to an intense attention to some religious subject which involves an alienation of the senses caused by God's action on the soul.[2] St Augustine gives just such an example,

> There are times when the soul is raptured into things seen that are similar to bodies, but are beheld in the spirit in such a way that the soul is totally removed from the bodily senses, more than in sleep but less than in death. By divine warning and assistance the soul knows that she does not behold bodies, but things like bodies seen in a spiritual way, just as people sometimes know they are dreaming even before they awake.[3]

St Hildegard of Bingen (1098–1179) describes a typical vision:

> My spirit ascends into the height of the firmament and the shifting air, and it spreads itself abroad among different peoples though they are in distant regions and places far from me. And because I see these things in such a manner, I therefore also behold them in changing forms of clouds and other created elements. But I do not hear them with my bodily ears, nor with my heart's thoughts, nor do I perceive them by the use of any of my five senses, but only in my soul, with my outer eyes open.[4]

We notice that there is 'suspension of the senses' but also the memory of the experience once the ecstasy has passed. St Teresa appears to downplay such extraordinary graces,

> Whatever [God] does the Lord unites it with himself but he makes it blind and dumb as he made St. Paul at his conversion, and so prevents it from having any sense of how or in what way that favour comes which it is enjoying; the great delight of which the soul is then conscious is the realization of its nearness to God.[5]

In her *Life* she records,

> I have been so completely beside myself that I have not known whether it has been a dream or whether the bliss that I have been experiencing has really come to me; and I have only known that it has not been a dream through finding myself bathed in tears.[6]

Hard-bitten misogynists will mutter that this is a woman's thing. Certainly such supernatural phenomena would seem to favour women far more than men (we have only to think of St Hildegard, St Catherine of Siena, St Catherine of Ricci, St Mary Magdalen of Pazzi, St Bridget of Sweden, St Faustina Kowalska, St Elizabeth of the Trinity and St Teresa herself). One might argue that women are more receptive and men more critical. But these are *not* consolations as in the earlier stages of prayer – to encourage us on the journey. It would seem that God uses them to reveals special secrets and in the process of the ecstasy makes the soul more capable to grasp them.[7] This extends to a comprehension of the very essence of God, according to St Thomas.[8]

St Teresa uses an example taken from the goldsmiths,

> For my own part I think his majesty is here enamelling gold which he has already prepared for this process by his gifts and has tested, by a thousand ways and means which the soul that has reached this state can describe, so as to discover how strong is the love which it bears him. This soul, which is the gold in question, remains all the time as motionless and as inert as if it were really gold; and the Divine Wisdom, well pleased to see it so, since so few love him with such strength, continues to set in the gold many precious stones and much elaborately worked enamel.[9]

It is as if she is saying that this is the icing on the cake which makes the cake more appetizing.

The Church has always taken a very strict line with ecstasy because it has many counterfeit varieties. Vatican II says, 'Extraordinary gifts are not to be rashly sought after, nor is it from them that the fruits of apostolic labours are to be presumptuously expected.'[10] St Teresa refers to 'illusions or the results of melancholia'.[11] Certainly there have been many ecstatics from the time of Saul at Gibeah (1 Sam 10:10f) to the convulsionaries of St Médard. It is noticeable that often no true recollection of the trance is retained nor were the messages either orthodox or coherent. True ecstasy can be tested against the level of spirituality, obedience to the rule of life, and the charity of the individual.

Revelations and visions

St Paul relates,

> I know someone in Christ who, fourteen years ago (whether in the body or out of the body I do not know, God knows), was caught up to the third heaven. And I know that this person (whether in the body or out of the body I do not know, God knows) was caught up into Paradise and *heard ineffable things* which no one may utter. (2 Cor 12:2)

St Teresa talks in terms of a celestial internet,

> The position seems to me to be that the Lord's will is for the soul to have at any rate some idea of what is happening in heaven, and, just as souls in heaven understand one another without speaking (which I never knew for certain till the Lord in His goodness willed me to see it and revealed it to me in a rapture), even so it is here.[12]

The communication of such truths can be by visions, words (locutions) or a simple apprehension of the truth, according to St Alphonsus Liguori.[13]

It would seem that visions and private revelations can occur at any time – within prayer, during ecstasy or sometimes when one is recollected and alone. They can last a moment or several days 'and even sometimes for a Year'.[14] Catherine Emmerich saw her visions of the Passion of Christ unroll in cinematic form. St John says,

> When these visions occur, it is as if a door opened into a most marvelous light, whereby the soul sees, as men do when the lightning suddenly flashes in a dark night. The lightning makes surrounding objects visible for an instance, and then leaves them in obscurity, though the forms of them remain in the imagination.[15]

Exactly what is the nature of a vision? St Teresa says that it is the most glorious image and then corrects what she has said, 'It must not be supposed that one looks at it as at a painting; it is *really alive, and sometimes speaks to the soul* and shows it things both great and secret.[16] If it is from God it will result in great joy, sweetness, love, humility, and a raising of the mind to God; whereas if it is not from God and either from our psychoses or, heaven forbid, from diabolic influence, then we will have dryness of spirit and self-exaltation.'[17] As ever 'By their fruits you will know them' (Matt. 7:20). In the case of St Bernadette, nobody could shift her from her insistence that she had seen the Mother of God at Massabielle in 1858, even under the most ferocious questioning from the Public Prosecutor and the Police Commissioner and under the threat of internment in a mental institution. In his questioning, the Commissioner asked Bernadette, 'This lady appeared at the back of the grotto?' 'Not at all: above the bush.' 'That her hair hung down behind like a veil?' 'I said she had a veil, it was white and very long ... Her hair could scarcely be seen.' 'That she had a yellow rose in her sash?' 'I said she has a blue sash, and there's no rose in her sash: there's a yellow rose on each foot.'[18] She always kept tenaciously to her original account. St Teresa maintains that it is of the essence of a true revelation that it comes with power and authority in itself and in the actions which follow.[19]

But it is not necessary to have visions to advance on the journey of prayer. We should not be scandalized by them but we should not put too much credit on them either. St John of the Cross is quite emphatic when he says,

> Let confessors direct their penitents into [the night of] faith, advising them frankly to turn away their eyes from all such things, teaching them how to void the desire and the spirit of them so that they may make progress, and giving them to understand how much more precious in God's sight is one work or act of the will performed in charity than are all the visions and communications that they may receive from heaven.[20]

To desire visions and revelations is the height of pride. St Philip Neri wrote, 'One must have humility, total submission to God and complete detachment from self in order not to lose God on account of visions.'[21] Dom David Knowles would seem to discount any mystical experience when he says,

> So far from being regarded as marvelous and supernatural, vision and locutions of a definite, communicable kind are the weak outward signs, or the only and inadequate appearance, of what could in itself have been a deeper enrichment of the soul.[22]

Ecclesiastical authorities could be said to permit private revelations rather than promote them because private revelations are not part of the deposit of faith.[23] There is always an element which is strictly personal. Bernadette declared that the lady had given her three secrets which she would only reveal 'if the Blessed Virgin told me to do so'.[24] It never happened. But Bernadette accepted from the beginning the truth of the revelation and acted upon it, telling the clergy that there was a call to penance and they should come in procession. Lourdes is the result ...

Any revelation which is contrary to dogma or morals must be rejected but also when a private revelation becomes public there is always the question of the accuracy of transmission. Fortunately Bernadette never wavered in her account. But there is always the possibility that the imagination may play tricks and zealous friends may add a commentary which becomes incorporated into the original message.

Intellectual revelations

As far as *intellectual* revelations (or locutions) are concerned, these are produced directly into the mind. St John describes the process,

> In certain cases the mind puts together so much to the purpose, and with such facility and clearness discovers by reflection things it knew not before (or that it had forgotten), that it seems to itself as if it was not itself which did so, but some third person which addressed it interiorly, reasoning, answering, and informing ... Thus the mind addresses itself to itself as if to some other person.[25]

The safe guide in all this, says St Teresa, is to leave oneself in the hands of God, 'whose words are works'.[26] The saint herself seemed to be in almost daily communication with Jesus, 'At other times, if the Lord spoke only one word to me (if, for example, as on the occasion I have already described, he said no more than "Be not troubled: have no fear."'[27] But there were other times when it was as if Teresa was having a discussion with herself about her problems and sharing them with Jesus.

When she was worried about the building of the convent of St Joseph of Avila the Lord said to her, 'I have already told you to go in as best you can', and then added, 'Oh the greed of mankind! So you think that there will not be enough ground for you! How often did I sleep all night in the open air because I had not where to lay my head!' Teresa adds somewhat charmingly, 'This amazed me, but I saw that he was right.'[28] How far does the individual contribute to locutions? In the case of successive locutions (which applies especially to St Teresa) the individual seems to be formulating ideas and reasoning things out,

> Proceeding thought by thought, forming precise words and judgments, deducing and discovering such unknown truths, with so much ease and clarity, that it will seem to him he is doing nothing and that another person is interiorly reasoning, answering and teaching him. Indeed, there is every reason for this belief, since he reasons with himself and replies as if carrying on a dialogue. In a way he really is speaking with another for, though he reasons by using his intellect as the instrument, the Holy Spirit frequently helps him to form these true concepts, words, and judgements, and thus he utters them to himself as though to another person.[29]

Thus, St John's clinical analysis of Teresa's 'conversations'.

Other mystical phenomena

There are other more extraordinary expressions which provided a certain morbid fascination: stigmata, bilocation and levitation. Two of these were combined in the person of St Pius of Pietrelcina (1887–1968), Padre Pio, the capuchin Franciscan.

True stigmata proceed from a supernatural cause, although psychiatrists admit that the human imagination is capable of producing such pains and wounds.[30] The appearance of the stigmata is usually instantaneous, located in the places in which tradition places the five wounds of Christ, and they often bleed on the days associated with his Passion. Authentic stigmatists seek to conceal their wounds and ask God to remove them. At death, they often disappear.

Padre Pio's bilocation is well attested. One or other of the appearances would take the form of a vision since physical bodies cannot be present in two places at the same time. His appearances were in most cases in answer to prayer. Why he was gifted with such phenomena remains uncertain although there was no doubt about his special contemplative union with God.

Levitation

The phenomena of levitation was witnessed by Brother Leo in the case of St Francis of Assisi and in the life of St Joseph of Cupertino (1603–1663) as well as in that of St John of the Cross by St Teresa herself. St Teresa used to refer to such incidents as 'spiritual visitations'. Adherents of Transcendental Meditation and many Eastern gurus levitate for short periods and Daniel Dunglas Home, the spiritualist, claimed in 1868 to have floated out of the upstairs window of Lord Adare's house at 5 Buckingham Gate and in through another – but there were no witnesses.[31] Robert Browning mocked the event in his portrayal of 'Mr Sludge the Medium'. Instead of obsessing over such phenomena, we ought to bear in mind the words of the Buddha to his disciples, 'they are a means to an end, not an end in themselves'.[32] The end for Christians is union with God, not the incidentals of the journey, as St Teresa points out, 'If only we knew him, we should love him in the same way in this world, and although not so perfectly as in heaven, yet very differently from what we do now.'[33]

Notes
1. Ponnelle & Bordet, p. 124.
2. Poulain, p. 243.
3. *Genesis ad Litteram*, Book 12, 26.
4. *Letter 103R to Guibert of Gembloux* in 1075.
5. *Interior Castle*, 7, 1. Bellini portrays an ecstatic Teresa in the Church of Santa Maria della Vittoria in Rome.
6. *Life*, chapter 18.
7. Poulain, p. 244. 'You have hidden these things from the learned and clever *and revealed* them to mere children' (Matt 11:25).
8. *Summa Theologica*, 2-2 q. 175 a 3.
9. *Conception of the Love of God*, chapter 6.
10. *Lumen Gentium* (Vatican 2: On the Church), n. 12.
11. *Conception of the Love of God*, chapter 6.
12. *Life*, chapter 27.
13. *Homo Apostolicus*, Appendix 1, n. 22.
14. *Interior Castle*, 6, 8.
15. *Ascent of Mount Carmel*, Book 2, 24.
16. *Interior Castle*, 6, 9.
17. *Ascent of Mount Carmel*, Book 2, 24.
18. Trochu, *Bernadette*, p. 85.
19. *Interior Castle*, 4, 5.
20. *Ascent of Mount Carmel*, Book 2, 22; St Bernard says, 'I have no desire for visions of dreams ... Jesus himself outshines them all.' *Commentary on the Song of Songs*, n. 2.
21. *Letter to Frederick Borromeo*, quoted in Turks, p. 98.
22. Knowles, *What is Mysticism*, p. 55.
23. *Catechism of the Catholic Church*, n. 67.
24. *Sayings of Bernadette*, p. 29.
25. *Ascent of Mount Carmel*, Book 2, 29.
26. Aumann, p. 428.

27. Harrison, pp. 2.22.
28. *Life*, chapter 33.
29. Aumann, pp. 427–8; *Ascent of Mount Carmel*, Book 2, 29.
30. Aumann, p. 433.
31. Harrison, p. 14.
32. *Mircea Eliade*, p. 5.
33. *Way of Perfection*, chapter 30.

Chapter 11

A Wondrous Journey

It is evident that the heights of prayer will be scaled by relatively few. Fewer still may hope for mystical experiences, but the mountain of prayer itself is open to all. We must truly *want* to pray, and we must believe in the One to whom we pray and not merely indulge in wishful thinking. Prayer is a *work* (like draughtsmanship or surgery); it demands a commitment of mind and heart.

We need to fix a time each day if at all possible. Brother Lawrence, it is true, thought that he could possess God and be in great peace 'as if he was in church' amid the noise and clatter of his kitchen. But for most of us there is a need to withdraw to one's secret place.

We can start by meditating on the words of Scripture, short phrases or prayers or incidents, not neglecting the Psalms, which Newman called 'that wonderful manual of prayer and praise, which from the time when its varied portions were first composed down to the last few centuries, has been the most precious viaticum of the Christian mind in its journey through the wilderness'.[1] These are the kindling for the fire – the means to prompt prayer in us.

But we must persevere when the going is hard.

Newman points out, 'It is not easy to keep the mind from wandering in prayer, to keep out all intrusive thoughts about other things. It is not at all easy to realize what we are about, who is before us, what we are seeking ...'[2]

At the same time it is important to remember that the Holy Spirit is the principal mover in all this. Even our desire to pray is due to his influence in us, and the journey itself is under his guidance. We must not start ticking off the stages of the journey and checking the state of our spiritual temperature. Instead we need to surrender ourselves to God for 'The Lord does not look so much at the magnitude of anything we do, as at the love with which we do it.'[3]

When Jesus preached his parables about the seed, he remarked that 'the crop sprouts and grows, without any knowledge of his' (Mark 4:27). It is the same with prayer, and some produces thirty-fold, some sixty-fold and some a hundred-fold (Matthew 13:8). The assimilation of God's word varies with each individual but given the right intention prayer will have even a quite dramatic impact. We will feel its effects in the first place in the tranquility it brings to us, 'If we fear we are doing nothing in our prayer, we are doing no small thing by pacifying the soul and bringing it into calm and peace.'[4] But there is also the increase of faith and love, 'when the soul not only desires the honour of God but really strives for it, and employs the memory and understanding in considering how it may please him and show its love for him more and more'.[5]

In case we begin to think that this is spiritual selfishness, we ought to consider that our journey of prayer should never be regarded as an exercise in self-improvement. Prayer always has that added dimension because we pray in communion with all those who are gathered into the household of God which is the Church, and so surrounded 'by a great cloud of witnesses' (Heb 12:1). We may not be conscious of this, but it is something tangible for those who have experienced the pain of isolation, torture and persecution. That is the reality of the Communion of Saints.

But prayer is also that unseen contribution to the spiritual dignity of our society. Cardinal Wright, when he was talking to the Bridgetine nuns in Rome, put it succinctly,

> It is impossible to programme into the computers the spiritual generosity, the piety, the austerity of the people; yet the well-being of the nations depends on these even more than it does on economic resources or political strategies.[6]

It is the absence of any spiritual dimension that is the cause of such great emptiness and inner loathing which manifests itself in increasing violence, degradation and despair. On the other hand we will never know the force for good which our prayer unleashes because it appeals directly to the One who makes all creation new.

In prayer we are not attempting merely to encounter a deeper self or a God within but to bring ourselves into contact with a God who is beyond our imagining and is the Lord of all. Christians believe that this supreme and almighty God has become visible and touchable in his Son. Through him we can know the Creator of all things. Through him we enter beyond the veil, into the darkness that leads to eternal light. Jesus willed to take on our humanity, to give value to our strivings. He took on himself the burden of our weaknesses and our sins so that we could live no longer for ourselves but for him. He prayed to the point of anguish so that we could persevere.

He climbed the wood of the Cross which was to lead to his glory so that we could climb the mountain of prayer with him, grieving for our sins, but conscious of his triumphant love and mercy. St Teresa remarks, 'Those who are faithful to prayer find themselves, they know not how, reaching the summit of the mountain where they meet God.'[7]

We are constantly being reminded of the places we should visit before we die. It would be a tragedy if in the race to visit ever more exotic locations, we neglected to make the journey that never ends – that of prayer, 'Happy is he, who, like Ulysses, has taken a wondrous journey.'[8]

Notes
1. *Historical Sketches*, vol. 2, p. 459.
2. *Parochial & Plain Sermons*, vol. 4, p. 75.
3. *Interior Castle*, 7, 3.
4. *Ascent of Mount Carmel*, 2, 15.
5. *Interior Castle*, 5, 4.
6. Quoted in *L'Osservatore Romano*, 25 October 1973.
7. *Way of Perfection*, chapter 12.
8. Joachim du Bellay, *Les Regrets*, 31.

Select Bibliography

Abhisktananda, *Prayer*, SPCK, London, 1972.
Augustine, St, *Confessions*, tr. F. Sheed, Sheed & Ward, 1960.
Aumann, J., *Spiritual Theology*, Sheed & Ward, 1986.
Bange, G., *Eastern Vessels, The Practice of Personal Prayer according to The Patristic Tradition*, tr. M. J. Miller, Ignatius Press, San Francisco, 2002.
Benedict, St, *Rule*, tr. D. Parry, Darton, Longmann & Todd, 1984.
Bernadette. Some Sayings of, Archives of Nevers, 1978.
Bernadin, J. L., *The Gift of Peace*, Loyola, Chicago, 1997.
Blackney, R. B. (ed.), *Meister Eckhart, A Modern Translation*, Harper & Row, New York, 1941.
Bouyer, L., *The Word, Church and Sacrament*, Geoffrey Chapman, London, 1961.
Brodrick, J., *Robert Bellarmine 1542–1621*, Longmans, Green & Co., London, 1950.
Camus. J-P., *The Spirit of St François de Sales*, tr. C. F. Kelley, Longmans, Green & Co., London, 1953.
Chaumant, H., *Directions spirituelles de St. François de Sales*, De l'Oraison, 1876.

Chinigo, M. (ed), *Teachings of Pope Pius XII*, Methuen, London, 1958.

Cross, F. L. and Livingstone, E. A., *The Oxford Dictionary of the Christian Church* (2nd edn), Oxford University Press, 1974.

D'Agnel, A., *St Vincent de Paul, Directeur de Conscience*, Tequi, Paris, 1925.

Effie in Venice – Unpublished Letters of Mrs John Ruskin written from Venice 1849–1852, John Murray, London, 1963.

Eliade, M., *Pantanyali & Yoga*, Schocken, New York, 1975.

Escrivá, J., St, *The Way*, Scepter, New York, 1982.

Fanning, S., *Mystics of the Christian Tradition*, Routledge, London, 2001.

Friends of God, Scepter 1986.

Gleason, R. W. (ed.), *The Spiritual Exercises of St Ignatius*, Image, New York, 1964.

Goodier, A., *Ascetical & Mystical Theology*, Burns & Oates, London, 1938.

Grou, J. N., *How to Pray*, Burns & Oates, London, 1965.

—— *Manual for Interior Souls*, St Anselm's Society, London, 1890.

Harrison, T., *The Marks of the Cross. The Story of Ethel Chapman*, Darton, Longman & Todd, London, 1981.

Hertz, J. H., *Daily Prayer Book*, Socino Press, London, 1976.

James, W., *The Varieties of Religious Experience*, Fontana, London, 1982.

John of the Cross, *Collected Works*, trs K. Kavanagh & O. Rodriguez, Nelson, London, 1964.

Johnston, W., *Silent Music*, Collins, London, 1974.

Julian of Norwich, *Showings of Love*, tr. J. Holloway, Liturgical Press, Minn., 2003.

Jung, C. G., 'Dogma & Natural Symbols' in Jung, G., *Collected Works*, vol. 11, Princeton University Press, New Jersey, 1969.

Knowles, D., *What is Mysticism?* Sheed & Ward, London, 1971.

—— *English Mystical Tradition*, Harper & Row, New York, 1971.

Knox R. & Oakley M. (trs), *The Imitation of Christ*, Burns Oates, London 1959.

Lassale, E., *El Zen*, Mensajero, Bilbao, 1977.

Lawrence, Br. (Nicholas Herman), *Practice of the Presence of God* [and other writings], tr. E. M. Blaiklock, Hodder, London, 1981.

Lercaro, G., *Methods of Mental Prayer*, tr. T. F. Lindsay, Burns & Oates, London, 1957.

Liguori, Alphonsus, *Works*, 15 vols, Isola del Liri, 1933.

Lossky, V., *In the Image & Likeness of God*, Mowbrays, London, 1976.

Macklem, M., *God Have Mercy: The Life of John Fisher of Rochester*, Oberon Press, Ottawa, 1967.

Mantzaridis, G., *The Deification of Man*, St Vladimir Press, Crestwood, NY, 1984.

Marmion, C., *Christ, the Life of the Soul*, Sands, London, 1925.

Merton, T., *The Ascent to Truth*, Burns & Oates, London, 1976.

Meschler, M., *The Book of Spiritual Exercises of St Ignatius*, 2 vols, Turin, 1934.

Meyendorff, J., *Byzantine Theology*, Mowbrays, London, 1974.

Nau, F., *Apophtegmes des Pères: Collections systématiques* (ed. Goy J-C), S.C. 387, Paris, 1993.
Newman, J. H., *Anglican Difficulties 2*, Longmans, Green & Co., London, 1918.
—— *The Arians of the Fourth Century*, Longmans, Green & Co., 1888.
—— *Essay on the Development of Christian Doctrine*, Longmans, Green & Co., London, 1885.
—— *Historical Sketches*, Longmans, Green & Co., 1902.
—— *Meditations & Devotions*, Longmans, Green & Co., 1885.
—— *Parochial & Plain Sermons*, Longmans Green & Co., 1911.
O'Neill, C., *Meeting Christ in the Sacraments*, Mercier Press, Cork, 1966.
Palmer, G., Sherrard, P.,Ware, K. (eds), *The Philokalia*, 4 vols, Faber, London, 1984.
Ponnelle, L., and Bordet, L., *Philip Neri & The Roman Society of His Times*, Sheed & Ward, London, 1937.
Poulain, A., *The Graces of Interior Prayer*, B. Herder, St Louis, 1908.
Pourrat, P., *Christian Spirituality*, tr. W. H. Mitchell, Burns & Oates, London, 1924.
Raguin, Y., *How to Pray Today*, Anthony Clarke, Wheathampstead, 1974.
Rumi, *The Essential Rumi*, ed. C. Barks, Harper, San Francisco, 1995.
Rutherford, A., *Acts for Mental Prayer*, Darton, Longman & Todd, London, 1961.
de Sales, Francis, *Introduction to the Devout Life*, tr. M. Day, Burns & Oates, London, 1959.
Scripta de San Ignacio, 2 vols, 1904.

Smith, A. (ed.), *Philokalia: The Eastern Churches Spiritual Texts*, Skylight, Vermont, 2006.
Smith, H., *The World's Religions*, Harper, San Francisco, 1991.
Squire A., *Asking the Fathers*, SPCK, London, 1975.
—— *Aelred of Rievaulx*, SPCK, London, 1969.
Staniforth, M. (tr.), *Early Christian Writings*, Penguin, London, 1981.
Tauler, J., *Spiritual Conferences*, trs E. College and Sr M. Jane, Tan, Rockford, Ill., 1961.
Teresa of Avila, St, *Complete Works*, tr. E. A. Peers, Sheed & Ward, London, 1978.
Theoleptos of Philadelphia, *Life and Letters*, ed. A. Hero, Hellenic College Press, Brookline, Mass., 1994.
Thérèse of Lisieux, *Autobiography of a Saint*, tr. R. Knox, Harvill, London, 1958.
Thérèse St. By Those who Knew Her, ed. C. Mahony, Veritas, Dublin, 1974.
Thomas of Jesus, CS, *La parte migliore ossia la vita contemplative*, ed. B. Ignazio di S Anna, Milan, 1930.
Thurston, H., *The Physical Phenomena of Mysticism*, Burns & Oates, London, 1951.
Tissot, Y., *L'Art d'utiliser ses fautes d'après S. François de Sales*, 1878.
Trochu, F., *St Bernadette Soubirous*, tr. J. Joyce, Longmans, Green & Co., London, 1958.
—— *The Curé of Ars*, tr. E. Graf, Burns & Oates, London, 1950.
Turks, P., *Philip Neri The True Face of Joy*, T & T Clarke, Edinburgh, 1995.
Vaggagini, C., *Theological Dimensions of the Liturgy*, tr. L. Doyle and W. Jurgens, Liturgical Press, Collegeville, Minn., 1976.

Velocci, G., *Prayer in Newman*, tr. N. L. Gregoris, Gracewing, Leominster, 2006.
Veuillot, P., *The Catholic Priesthood*, 2 vols, Gill, Dublin, 1957.
Ward, B., *The Desert Fathers,* Penguin, London, 2003.
Ware, K., *The Orthodox Way*, Mowbrays, London, 1979.
—— *The Orthodox Church*, Penguin, London, 1981.
Wolters, C. (tr.), *The Cloud of Unknowing & Other Works*, Penguin, London, 1978.

Appendix 1

Meditation Methods

A. *St Ignatius' Method*
1. Preparation of points (the night before) with reconsideration in the morning.
2. Put oneself in the presence of God – act of adoration
3. Preludes
   – historical: recollection of the event to be meditated
   – imaginative: composition of place
   – petition: asking for the particular grace
4. Meditation
   – exercise of the memory: recollection
   – exercise of the intellect: make the material one's own
       draw practical conclusions
       make acts of praise, love etc.
5. Conclusions
   – colloquy
   – Our Father, Hail Mary, etc.
6. After meditation: examen on the success or failure

B. *Carmelite Method*
1. Preparation
    - removing obstacles: distractions and disordered affections, mortification of the senses
    - exercise of the presence of God
2. Reading
    - the material for the meditation; recalling to mind some truth or aspect of God's Love
3. Imaginative representation
    - reconstructing the event or mystery
4. Meditation or Consideration
    - the goal is to understand God's love for us
5. The Affective Colloquy
    - responding to God's love
6. Thanksgiving
    - 'The mercies of God I will sing forever'
7. Oblation
    - offering of oneself to God
    - a definite resolution to apply our prayer to our life
8. Petition
    - for our own sanctification and for the needs of others
    - acts of contrition, humility and the love of God

C. *St Francis de Sales' Method*
1. Preparation of material
    - reading and arranging points for meditation
2. Exercise the Presence of God
    - God is everywhere and in everything
    - God is in your heart and soul
    - Christ abides with his children on earth
    - Christ is present in his humanity, especially in the Eucharist

3. Invocation
   - Act of adoration
   - Prayer – asking to serve God in this meditation
   - Prayer to our guardian angel and the saints
   - Resolution to accept all the obstacles during the course of this meditation 'as though they had been so many consolations and so much peace'.
4. Composition of Place
   - Exercise of the mind: considerations actual meditation
   - Exercise of the will
     a) Love of God and neighbour, desire for heaven, imitation of Christ's life, hatred of sin,
        confidence in God's love and his mercy, etc.
     b) Colloquy
     c) Resolutions – practical and particular
5. Conclusions
   - Act of Thanksgiving
   - Act of Oblation – offering of oneself to God
   - Our Father; Hail, Mary
6. After Meditation
   - spiritual bouquet/nosegay – a 'taste' of the meditation
   - recollection to retain the feelings entertained in prayer and to accustom oneself to pass from prayer to action.
   - resolutions to be put into practice during the day.

D. *John Henry Newman's Method*
   - for saying the rosary:
       Try it thus, if you don't so use it at present, but

perhaps you do; – viz. Before each mystery, set before you a picture of it and fix your mind upon that picture, (e.g. the Annunciation, the Agony, etc.) *while* you say the *Pater* and 10 *Aves*, not thinking of the words, only saying them correctly. Let the exercise be hardly more than a meditation. Perhaps this will overcome any sense of tedium.

Letter to George Ryder, 19 September 1848
Letters and Diaries of John Henry Newman,
vol. 12, p. 263.

Appendix 2

Prayers before Prayer

Prayer to the Holy Spirit
Come, Holy Spirit, fill the hearts of your faithful and kindle in them the fire of your love. Send forth your Spirit and they shall be created and you shall renew the face of the earth.

Prayer of St Augustine
Lord Jesus, let me know myself, let me know you and desire nothing else but only you. Let me hate myself and love you, and do all things for the sake of you. Let me humble myself and exalt you and think of nothing but only you. Let me die to myself and live in you and take whatever happens as coming from you. Let me forget myself, and walk after you and ever desire to follow you.

Prayer of Archbishop Goodier
Jesus Christ, close beside me, here and now, the same now as in Jerusalem and Galilee, looking at me with your loving eyes, longing to have me for your very own. Feeling for me with your tender heart, desiring to give me what is best for me, yet meek and humble, waiting for me.

Prayer of St Anselm
Lord our God, grant us grace to desire you with our whole heart, that so desiring we may seek and find you; and finding you we may love you; and loving you we may hate those sins from which you have redeemed us; for the sake of Jesus Christ.

Prayer of Cardinal Newman
Dear Jesus, Come into me and make my whole being so completely yours that all my life may shine like yours. Shine through me and stay in me in such a way that every soul I meet may feel your presence in my soul. Let them look up and see no longer me, but only Jesus.

Prayer of St Thomas More
O Lord, give us a mind that is humble, quiet, peaceful, patient and charitable, and a taste of your Holy Spirit in all our thoughts words, and deeds. Give us a lively faith, a firm hope, a fervent charity and love of you. Take from us all lukewarmness in meditation and all dullness in prayer. Give us fervour and delight in thinking of you, your grace, and your tender compassion toward us. Give us, good Lord, the grace to work for the things we pray for. Amen.